Seventy-Five Years of The Curtis Institute of Music

A Narrative Portrait by Diana Burgwyn

"To hand down through contemporary

masters the great traditions of the past.

To teach students to build

on this heritage for the future."

Josef Hofmann, Director (1927–1938)

One of The Institute's greatest strengths is communication between generations.
Here, pianist alumnus/faculty member Peter Serkin
greets his former teacher Mieczyslaw Horszowski.

Seventy-Five Years of The Curtis Institute of Music

A Narrative Portrait by Diana Burgwyn

1924–1999

The Curtis Institute of Music and the author have made all attempts to insure that the events and people described in this book were portrayed faithfully.
However, as the sources included occasionally conflicting archival materials, as well as the recollections of individuals, there may be inaccuracies.

This book was designed by Art 270, Inc., and edited by Ann E. Diebold of The Curtis Institute of Music. The cover photograph is by Brownie Harris.
The text was set in Adobe Goudy. The book was printed using 300 line screen duotones by
The Stinehour Press of Lunenburg, Vermont, on Mohawk Superfine White Smooth, 100 pound text.
The binding is by Acme Bookbinding of Charlestown, Massachusetts. This book was printed in an edition of seven thousand copies.

Acknowledgments

The Curtis Institute of Music is grateful to the following people who graciously shared their time and knowledge in the development and production of this book:

A. Margaret Bok, Vera Bruestle, Anthony Checchia, Peter Checchia, Orlando Cole, Richard Doran, Robert Fitzpatrick, Steven Hegarty, Samantha Kelly, James R. Ledwith, Esq., James Meyer, Esq., Dianne Mill, David Morris, Jayne Nishimura, Anne O'Donnell, Letizia Paganini, Terri Skelton, Sue Ströhm and Elizabeth Walker.

Table of Contents

FOREWORD

The occasion of a seventy-fifth-year anniversary affords The Curtis Institute of Music an opportunity to look back to the beginning and reflect on what has happened over the decades. For three-quarters of a century Curtis has been synonymous with the finest musical training and the highest level of musical performance. Worldwide, musicians look to Curtis to produce the most promising, talented and dedicated young artists, who in their careers will celebrate and sustain the grand tradition of musical performance. We are fortunate to be a part of an organization where great talents come together to help each other flourish, where students and faculty are wholly dedicated to continuing and strengthening our musical heritage.

The text that follows tells the story of The Curtis Institute of Music. It is not a "history," but rather an attempt to bring our beloved Institute to life as it was seventy-five years ago and to show how it developed over the years: to describe the personalities, the performances, the long-held customs, the outside events that affected it, even its quirks. This book is in a sense a portrait from the past to the present. We hope that those who are part of the Curtis family will find that it meshes with and brings to mind their own special memories.

Milton L. Rock
Chairman of the Board of Trustees

A few moments of relaxation in front of Curtis between the intense hours of study and music-making (1998).

Introduction

Theme and Variations

Wednesday afternoon tea, held in the Common Room,
is a cherished Curtis tradition dating back to the school's earliest years (1994).

It is three o'clock on a Wednesday afternoon, time for the weekly Curtis Institute of Music tea. The tradition dates back to the 1920s, when the school's founder, Mary Louise Curtis Bok, presided over an elegant bone china tea service, greeting every student by name. It's not much different now. Naomi Graffman, wife of the current president/director, pianist Gary Graffman, knows all the students too, as did previous Curtis First Ladies Andrea de Lancie and Irene Serkin. Like her predecessors, Mrs. Graffman is seated in a tapestried armchair behind a huge brass samovar, a treasured relic of old Russia. As the young musicians take their tea, they dive into a platter of her justifiably famous homemade brownies.

The setting is the Common Room, a huge foyer rising two-and-one-half stories in height, its walls and ceilings paneled in rich wood. A gilded grand piano stands in front of an ornate limestone mantelpiece, and Oriental carpeting, worn by decades of footsteps, adds a softening warmth.

It's a scene that would likely have pleased Mrs. Bok. She would have enjoyed the exchange of news between faculty and students — the awards won, competitions looming, student concerts played, recordings made, summer plans being hatched.

Admittedly, the students' attire would come as a surprise to her. No more starched shirts and three-piece suits, no cloche hats or silk stockings or white gloves. In the Common Room today, Mrs. Bok would spot a t-shirt reading "Go for Baroque," ponytails of all lengths on both sexes, and an assortment of jeans, tights, baggy knee-length sweaters and cowboy boots.

On the bulletin board she would see a formal invitation from the Graffmans, inviting the entire Curtis family to the annual black-tie holiday party. That, too, goes way back.

At The Curtis Institute of Music, traditions die hard.

Once again we are in the Common Room, on a bright Monday morning in February. The Institute is stirring to life, with students hauling in book bags and instrument cases of every size and condition. Much of their talk, which is in a variety of languages from Ukrainian to Mandarin Chinese, relates to the previous day's concert of the Curtis Symphony Orchestra at Philadelphia's Academy of Music.

The program had been stamped with the Curtis imprimatur, for it included the cello concerto by graduate Samuel Barber with another graduate, Wendy Warner, as soloist, as well as a contemporary piece by Richard Danielpour, newly appointed to the faculty.

Also on the program was John Corigliano's Symphony No. 1, a moving work dedicated to friends who died in the AIDS epidemic. At the very end of the last movement, during a long and difficult pianissimo solo for a cellist, a loud cough had erupted in the hall, causing the student's bow to lose contact with the cello string. She is in the Common Room now, talking about the lapse. What had been upsetting the previous day is now almost humorous — the realities of performance.

Everyone agrees that the concert was a decided success, with the audience displaying an enthusiasm rare for a program of entirely twentieth-century music.

"I don't think I've ever heard a more moving concert," says the chair of the school's liberal arts department, Joan Landis, to some of the players.

Curtis students, trombonist Joseph McEttrick and hornist Andrew Karr, at a Wednesday afternoon tea (1997).

Members of the horn section of the Curtis Symphony Orchestra perform at the Academy of Music. Pictured, left to right, are Michal Emanovsky, Gabriel Kovach, Adam Iascone and Ross Pekar (1999).

Tradition and innovation: twin values that have kept The Curtis Institute of Music on course during its venerable life. Go to any lesson, any class, and you'll see it in action. This one, for instance:

A CD is blaring forth with distinctly atonal sounds as the students file in to Jennifer Higdon's Tuesday afternoon class on twentieth-century music.

"Name the composer in three words or less," says Ms. Higdon to the group of twelve, most of them American-born. A 1988 Curtis graduate with a Ph.D. in composition from the University of Pennsylvania, she is a recent Guggenheim Award recipient.

"We need a clue," responds one student.

"Well, it's an American composer."

"Living or dead?"

"Dead. But he was living when he wrote it."

"Elliott Carter?"

"No."

"Philip Glass?"

"No."

Nor Sessions nor Shapey. Eventually they run out of names, and Ms. Higdon tells the students the piece is by Aaron Copland.

"Nah!" There is a communal sense of disbelief.

She follows with background on Copland, who began writing at a time when there was no music that could be characterized as "American." She passes out scores, and the students talk about what makes Copland Copland: the open intervals, the predominance of brass, the high tessitura, the transparency of orchestration.

Some like his music, others not. One in the latter camp opines, "I think Copland was revered because America was searching for a sound of its own."

That discussion broadens into more thorny questions. Why does every composer have to be great — isn't it okay to just be doing a good job? And were Bach and Mozart less inspired because their work was commissioned?

Then, of course, that old desert island question: which composer would you take if you could only take one?

"If I were stuck on a desert island and had to choose between Brahms and Copland," says Jennifer Higdon, "I'd take Copland."

"Singers are weird. We think differently, we act differently. Rejoice in that existence; don't try to prove you're normal," says baritone Thomas Hampson. He is speaking to the vocal students assembled in Curtis Hall, six of whom have been selected to sing for him in this master class.

Acting a part is not enough for Mr. Hampson; being the part is. "Go to the source, be the person, and sing the song," he tells the students. "What colors a human voice is the passion with which you imbue it."

After soprano Margarita Gomez performs an aria by Mozart, he questions her. "What does Elettra feel while she is singing this? Is she reflective? Joyful? Is she angry at someone? Is Elettra an angry person?"

Similarly, he probes the character of Lorelei in the Schubert song performed by bass Valeriano Lanchas. "Is this a real witch?" he asks. "Who is Lorelei? A bad dream or a physical witch person who comes to torment you?"

When he senses that Mr. Lanchas is not fully inhabiting the song, Mr. Hampson turns the student's back to the audience and has him sing it again. "Forget about the public," he advises. Then he slowly turns the singer to face the audience, shielding his eyes. Mr. Lanchas is no longer the onlooker; now he is the song.

Nothing escapes Mr. Hampson that might affect vocal tone. He works on "anchoring" the voice. He wants to know how a singer's left ankle feels. He has the group stomp on one foot and feel the stomp in the knees, hips, shoulders.

"Nice heels," he says, smiling, to soprano Sungji Kim, of her elegant footwear. "I'm gonna come back next time with an ax."

At the end of the session, which has gone over three hours without a break, Thomas Hampson is so delighted with the students' progress that he hugs the last singer and the afternoon's pianist, Danielle Orlando. Cheers and screams erupt from the audience.

Metropolitan Opera baritone and acclaimed recitalist Thomas Hampson gives student Valeriano Lanchas suggestions on interpreting a Schubert song (1997).

In addition to musical studies, Curtis students also participate in academic endeavors.
Pictured here is pianist Ieva Jokubaviciute (1998).

"What means 'homunculus?'" asks a Bulgarian voice student.

Teacher Mary-Jean Hayden provides a definition. It's a scientific term for "pygmy" that many Americans wouldn't know, but Ms. Hayden's class on "English as a Second Language" is made up of all non-Americans. Ranging in age from fourteen to twenty-four, they represent Bulgaria, China, Colombia, Korea and Ukraine.

From "neuron" to "antibodies" and "regeneration," the lesson proceeds with equally mystifying words and phrases encountered in daily conversation with fellow students. "Space case," for instance, or its synonym, "flake."

When the students began the class back in September, some were more proficient in English than others. But now all are able to communicate quite well.

Take Solomiya Ivakhiv, a violinist of seventeen. Six months ago, she says, about all she knew of English was: "Hello, my name is Solomiya."

Now, in class, she talks about her younger brother and her chemist father, both still in Ukraine. And about the fact that she and her mother, who has remained with her in Philadelphia, will return home for the summer.

Being able to speak English has helped overcome the loneliness.

Dvořák's rousing Carnival Overture *is threatening to burst the walls of Curtis Hall where, on a Saturday morning, about a hundred students are gathered, some pressed up against the walls with their instruments. They are straining to understand the northern British accent of their guest conductor, the irrepressible Simon Rattle.*

Sir Simon has been treating the occasion as if it were a professional recording session — complete with the presence of a nasty, if fictitious, recording producer who complains about every note and phrase. The purpose, of course, is to prepare the students for the rigors of a real recording session, which will not be far off for many of them.

Corrections and directives issue forth from the conductor. One phrase, he says, "sounds sort of dark and wodgy, like this room." And the rhythms in Bohemian music, which this is, should not be played in a rigid fashion but "bent." Restraint, he tells the students, is not a characteristic of this work; he gives the principal flutist "license to kill."

As for the cellos, in one passage they must play "like little devils in a Morse code machine." When a lackluster phrase emerges from the ensemble, he suggests that any shape will do "except for a sewing machine." Finally, Sir Simon advises the entire orchestra to take two weeks to study jazz singer Betty Carter.

When a first "take" is played back, the conductor hunches over his score, marking it with pencil and alerting the young musicians to a smoothly turned phrase, an incorrect intonation. Then he says "Now, let's make one for keeps!"

They do, and he is delighted with it. It's been a long morning, and everyone is wrung out — except, it seems, Sir Simon.

Sir Simon Rattle rehearses the Curtis Symphony Orchestra (1997).

Monteverdi's Coronation of Poppea *is presented in The Institute's black box theater, with Janelle Robinson and Nikola Mijailovic in leading roles (1994).*

"If we have a train wreck, I'll stop you," says stage director Chas Rader-Shieber to the singers gathered, with their ever-present bottles of water, in the intimate third-floor black box theater. "Otherwise, we'll fix it afterward."

It's a Saturday morning, time for a run-through of "Scenes of Love and Hate," which is to be staged four times on Valentine's Day weekend, and Mr. Rader-Shieber is ensconced at a long table with a yellow pad for note-taking.

"Shoes or shoeless?" asks one singer, referring to the newly painted floor. The floor is dry, responds the stage director, so shoes are fine. The set, by vocal arts administrator-cum-scenic-designer Ralph Batman, is a living room with Oriental rugs and furniture that look suspiciously as if they've been plucked from another Curtis location.

Danielle Orlando, musical director for the production, is at the piano, prepared to accompany the singers in a pastiche spanning 400 years of vocal music, as created by Mr. Rader-Shieber and Mikael Eliasen, head of the Curtis vocal studies department. It's all held together with one character, Richard Strauss' Ariadne, from the opera Ariadne auf Naxos, *who has been jilted by her lover and, in the setting of a cocktail party, gets a lot of advice about love in a variety of languages.*

The dizzying progression takes us from Ariadne's time back to the sixteenth century, where the vicious Poppea, singing the music of Claudio Monteverdi, is ready to kill (literally) for her man. And thence to Mozart's Papagena, who has been transformed from age eighty to eighteen in the blink of an eye. When all the guests have had their song, Ariadne, played by soprano Karen Slack, takes heart and decides to wait for "The Man I Love," courtesy of George Gershwin.

"Okay," says Mr. Rader-Shieber, the feared train wreck not having occurred. "Get your scores and gather round." He changes the action here and there, corrects the diction, reminds soprano Rachael Garcia to be sure she connects with countertenor Jeffrey Kim and not the magazine she's holding, and assures the group that the flowers, now false, will be real. The food, also real, will be finger food. There will be three "working" bottles of champagne, but #2 is to remain closed.

"Can we have real champagne?" someone asks.

"No. Sparkling cider."

"Cheesecake?"

"Maybe, if it doesn't crumble."

The next rehearsal will be tonight at six. Forget about an evening out.

It's ten o'clock on a weekday evening, and three Curtis students — piano, violin and trumpet — have just played in a recital, the thirty-fourth of the school year. Featured were works by Enesco, Tartini, Paganini, Bach and Debussy. The audience was full of faculty members, fellow students (who cheered and stomped their feet and whistled for the performers) and Philadelphia music lovers, including three generations of one family. Now everyone is spilling out into the Common Room, and the performers are accepting praise, dissecting problem areas and considering where to go for a pizza.

Audience member Farid Noor is leaving with his daughters, aged eight and nine. He's driven to Philadelphia from his home in Medford Lakes, New Jersey, to attend the free concert. The Noors are from Egypt and this is their second student recital. For Mr. Noor, Curtis is "a miracle."

Philadelphian Wesley Emmons, who is also departing, has been aware of that miracle for two decades. He is a regular at the Curtis student concerts, and he served on the board of directors of the Friends of Curtis. Mr. Emmons misses only about three evenings a year. "How many concerts does that add up to?" someone asks him. "About 1,750," he replies.

The corner of 18th and Locust Streets is now almost deserted, but the music does not end. In a practice room of The Curtis Institute of Music, a cello student works on a solo passage from Tchaikovsky's opera Eugene Onegin, *its poignant melody wafting on the cold February air.*

One of The Institute's many chamber music groups in performance at a student recital.
Pictured are violinists Nathan Cole and Zachary DePue, cellist Priscilla Lee and violist Jessica Thompson (1999).

Through the open windows of The Institute, the sounds of young musicians practicing can be heard (1995).

Mary Louise Curtis Bok.

Chapter One

The Early Years

FROM CASTLES IN SPAIN TO MANSIONS ON RITTENHOUSE SQUARE

She looks down upon The Curtis Institute of Music from many portraits and at different stages of life: a gracious woman of erect carriage and refined manners. Her features are even and delicate, her hair a light brown in youth, gradually turning to snow-white. The expression on her face is serene and rather prim, but one sees a hint of mischief in her dark, dancing eyes; a clarity of vision and purpose.

Mary Louise Curtis Bok had a privileged youth that in some ways made her an unlikely founder of The Curtis Institute, especially at a time when most women of her class presided over tea at home — not amidst a crowd of students at a conservatory. Yet her background prior to the opening of The Curtis Institute of Music in October 1924, when she was forty-eight, was an ideal preparation for her life's work. That work, providing a music education of uncompromising standards to highly gifted young people, became Mary Bok's overriding purpose in a life that lasted ninety-three years.

She was born on August 6, 1876, the only child of Cyrus H. K. Curtis and Louisa Knapp, an ambitious, religious and musically-inclined couple, originally of Portland, Maine, and later of Boston, who had met singing in a church choir. Cyrus Curtis traveled to Philadelphia that same year, when the nation was celebrating its centennial. So impressed was he with the city that he chose it as the location for his new business venture. The Curtis Publishing Company quickly became profitable, its founder a man of wealth and power. *The Saturday Evening Post* would soon be one of the most popular magazines in America, as would the *Ladies' Home Journal*, of which Louisa Knapp Curtis was named first editor.

Cyrus Curtis owned a fine pipe organ, which he enjoyed playing. His daughter studied both organ and piano. "Music," she would say many years later to students at The Curtis Institute, "beginning where speech leaves off, tells more of things human and divine, of nature,

Leopold Stokowski, with help from Thaddeus Rich, rehearses the Curtis Orchestra in the Common Room (1925).

Three pillars of The Institute, each an alumnus and faculty member:
Jascha Brodsky, violin; Vladimir Sokoloff, piano; and Orlando Cole, cello.

Three renowned violinists and a soprano take a swim. From left: Jascha Heifetz, Efrem Zimbalist, Alma Gluck and Fritz Kreisler.

life and love, than we can stammer in words, and tells it in a language that is universal and understandable to every human heart."

At the age of twenty, Mary Louise Curtis married Edward W. Bok, a young Dutch journalist whom her mother had chosen as her own successor to edit the *Journal*. Two sons were born of that marriage, Curtis, in 1897, and Cary, in 1905.

With an upbringing so directed to professional excellence, it was not surprising that Mrs. Bok would eventually look for her own niche. That was to be found, first, at the Settlement Music School on Christian Street in South Philadelphia. Settlement had been started in 1908 by two young women, Blanche Wolf Kohn and Jeanette Selig Frank, who hoped in this way to introduce the neighborhood's culturally and financially deprived children to the power and beauty of classical music. As part of her involvement with Settlement, Mrs. Bok organized fundraising events at the Curtis Publishing Company, featuring recitals by some of the best-known musicians of the day.

The Settlement School continued to grow in cramped quarters. In memory of Louisa Knapp, who had died in 1910, Mrs. Bok donated funds from her mother's estate for a new building. Gradually, she became aware that some of the children had sufficient talent for professional careers but were without the money needed for serious study, and so she helped to organize a conservatory division at Settlement. It followed that a separate school with rigorous standards of teaching and performance would be the wisest course, and Settlement's conservatory division would serve as its nucleus, with initial funding deriving from the remainder of Louisa Knapp's estate.

Past Meets Present

Leopold Stokowski, genius that he was in matters of technology, would have loved it:

The gift he made to Edward and Mary Louise Curtis Bok of Johann Sebastian Bach's Passacaglia in C minor, arranged and recorded by him for the Duo-Art Aeolian Pipe Organ, a reproducing organ piano roll, can now be heard in sound-byte form on the World Wide Web. The recording is part of the vast Stokowski Collection presented by The Curtis Institute of Music to the University of Pennsylvania in 1998, and it is the only known recording of Mr. Stokowski playing the organ.

The Common Room of The Institute set for a gala reception at the dedication of the recital hall (1927).

Seated at the harpsichord, Wanda Landowska with a group of Curtis students (1925/26 school year).

Mrs. Bok's dream of creating a new generation of American-born musical artists was shared by two men whose imprint upon the conservatory-to-be would be great. One was the Polish-born pianist Josef Hofmann, who had been the only private pupil of Anton Rubinstein. Mrs. Bok and her husband first met Mr. Hofmann on the pianist's second tour of the United States, at age twenty-two, after which he was their frequent house guest, setting up a workshop over the garage where he indulged his passion for scientific experimentation. At the time of The Institute's founding, he was in mid-career and shortly to become a U.S. citizen.

Thought by many to be the greatest pianist of his time, especially in the Romantic literature, Josef Hofmann played with an aristocratic, flowing tone, his sound sensuous and his technique brilliant. Though on stage he exhibited a jaunty manner, at heart he was a rather shy man with a rigidly disciplined mind, intense powers of concentration and a fierce passion for truth in life and music. He was also a composer and one of the first musicians of note to make recordings. What better choice to head the piano faculty at the emerging conservatory?

The other inspiration for Mrs. Bok was the glamorous, golden-haired conductor, Leopold Stokowski. Born in Britain but possessed of an imaginative, if inauthentic, eastern European accent, Mr. Stokowski had taken Philadelphia by storm as conductor of the Philadelphia Orchestra, which he transformed into one of the world's finest musical ensembles. A man of charisma and supreme confidence, he held strong opinions, which he did not hesitate to inflict upon others, including his audiences. Single-handedly, "Stoki," as he was sometimes known, propelled his ultra-traditional Philadelphia audiences into the music of their own time and demanded that they be attentive listeners.

Known to the Boks since his early days in Philadelphia, Mr. Stokowski was grateful for a long-term gift from an "unknown donor," later revealed to be Edward Bok, which helped his orchestra through a period of financial crisis. As for Mary Bok, she directed her prodigious energies to service on Mr. Stokowski's board of directors. There was a close friendship between the two — she called him "Prince" and he autographed photographs to her with that sobriquet.

"Many a time," wrote Mary Bok later, "our intimate group — my husband and I, and Mr. Hofmann or Mr. Stokowski — would sit together evenings and indulge in a sort of castle-in-Spain-building. We'd talk about how splendid it would be someday, somehow, to build here, in America, a conservatory that would assure these talented young people [from Settlement] really worthy instruction...."

Leopold Stokowski in his later years.

Eventually, castle-building became bricks and mortar of a more concrete sort. To house their new school, the Boks purchased three neighboring buildings on the south side of Locust Street next to the peaceful green oasis of Rittenhouse Square. These edifices had been among the most beautiful privately owned homes in Philadelphia. The main building, formerly the home of the prominent Drexel family and located at 1726 Locust Street, was rich

At The Institute's first commencement, held May 22, 1934, soprano Marcella Sembrich and pianist Leopold Godowsky are presented with honorary degrees by Mrs. Bok and Josef Hofmann.

in Romanesque and Renaissance architectural details. Its handsomely appointed reception area (now known as the Common Room) was set off by wood-paneled walls and ceilings and a carved limestone mantel, with a stained-glass skylight. Ceiling paintings of allegorical subjects (in what is now called the Bok Room) were by Edwin Blashfield, painted as a gift from the Drexels for Mrs. Bok when she bought the house. Ironwork was later added by the renowned Polish-born artisan Samuel Yellin.

The Sibley house, which adjoined the Drexel mansion to the south and which constituted the main entrance in the first years, was a gift to Mrs. Bok from her husband and father, who believed that one should not only buy the building one intended to use, but the one next to it. In this case, they could not have been more prescient. The third house was the Cramp mansion, located to the east side of the main building, an outstanding example of Beaux-Arts style, which was renamed Knapp Hall in honor of Mrs. Bok's mother.

The intrinsic beauty of the three buildings was enhanced by Mary Bok with elegant furniture and carefully chosen works of art, Oriental rugs and Gobelin tapestries. These would serve a purpose beyond their own beauty: as a fitting accompaniment to the music produced within and as an expression of gracious living to generations of young people, whose homes and families often were many miles, even continents, away.

One of Mrs. Bok's tasks was to find a director for the new enterprise. The man chosen was Johann Grolle, a Dutch-trained orchestra violinist associated with Settlement. Mr. Grolle was a Socialist; his admirable, if rather lofty, aim was the redemption of society through art. The first students — 203 the opening year — would derive mainly from Settlement, as would certain of the faculty members. A distinguished advisory committee of musicians and musicologists spread the word that The Curtis Institute of Music was looking for the finest student talent, regardless of financial status, and that applicants would be chosen through a rigidly applied audition process.

The Institute was chartered by the Commonwealth of Pennsylvania on April 18, 1924, not coincidentally the birthday of Leopold Stokowski (which birthday is another matter — in actuality, he was forty-two, but he had taken to lopping off five years). The charter declared the school's purpose succinctly: "To train exceptionally gifted young musicians for careers as performing artists on the highest professional level."

October 1, 1924, was to mark the official opening of The Curtis Institute of Music, but construction work on the buildings delayed this by almost two weeks. Onlookers were treated to quite a sight when, in early October, a parade of Steinway grand pianos emerged from huge trucks — "one of the largest shipments of pianos...ever to arrive in Philadelphia," noted a local newspaper. Finally, on October 13, the school opened its doors, its student body deriving from some twenty states of the U.S. as well as abroad.

Piano Questions Answered

Pianist Josef Hofmann had a connection with the Curtis Publishing Company that long predated the formation of The Curtis Institute of Music. This was through a column published regularly in the "Ladies' Home Journal" called "Piano Questions Answered," in which Mr. Hofmann responded to queries about piano-playing posed by the magazine's readers.

A gilded and decorated Steinway piano from the original Drexel mansion's drawing room is now housed in The Institute's main building (c.1900).

White Lilies-of-the-Valley and Purple Traffic Lights

That Mary Bok and her colleagues in castle-building managed to lure some of the world's leading musicians to the faculty is a tribute to their dedication and the astuteness of their plan. The presence of Leopold Stokowski and Josef Hofmann to head conducting and piano, respectively, did not hurt, either. Joining them were such figures as Marcella Sembrich, the Polish-born coloratura and former Metropolitan opera star; Hungarian violinist Carl Flesch, who had developed a famous teaching method; Carlos Salzedo, the French-born harpist and composer who single-handedly brought that instrument from the background of the orchestra to center-stage; and Rosario Scalero, Italian violinist and composer, who, over two decades, would teach many of The Institute's most gifted composition students.

Three of the world's most eminent pianists, Wilhelm Backhaus, Benno Moiseiwitsch and Moriz Rosenthal, came to the faculty within a short time of the school's founding. None remained for long, however, since, reportedly, Mr. Hofmann tended to give other pianists a hard time.

In 1927, Lea Luboshutz, the Odessa-born violinist who had studied with Eugène Ysaÿe and was a known recitalist and orchestra soloist, joined the faculty, remaining for two decades. A year later the violin faculty was enhanced by the arrival of two legendary figures who had left St. Petersburg after the Bolshevik Revolution: Leopold Auer and his former student, Efrem Zimbalist — the latter destined to be among the most important figures in the history of The Curtis Institute (as well as in the personal life of Mary Louise Curtis Bok).

For many decades, the Curtis String Quartet (violinists Jascha Brodsky and Charles Jaffe, cellist Orlando Cole and violist Max Aronoff) brought glory and appreciative new chamber music audiences to The Institute.

The beloved, if uncompromising, faculty member, Russian pianist Isabelle Vengerova (c. 1955).

Thanks in no small measure to the presence of Leopold Stokowski, several illustrious first-desk players of the Philadelphia Orchestra also joined the faculty. Among them were William Kincaid, flute; Marcel Tabuteau, oboe; Anton Horner, horn; Anton Torello, double bass; and Saul Caston, trumpet.

The instrumental curriculum included organ, taught by the distinguished Canadian musician Lynnwood Farnam, a renowned interpreter of Bach. Special courses on seventeenth- and eighteenth-century music were taught by Wanda Landowska, the great Polish-born harpsichordist and pianist. By 1929 students could even study campanology (carillon-playing) with the Belgian master Anton Brees. The six-week course took place at Edward Bok's Singing Tower in Lake Wales, Florida, a magnificent edifice of pink marble and coquina rock surrounded by a moat; visitors dubbed it "America's Taj Mahal."

Despite — or perhaps because of — the abundance of big names, it was not always smooth sailing between mentors and their protégés. Many of the faculty were new to teaching, having spent their professional lives performing. Since English was frequently not their native tongue, they resorted to using their limited vocabulary emphatically and, sometimes, with a tone of sarcasm. (One joker suggested that there should have been a course in remedial English for faculty.) And, because they were famous, they were accustomed to the royal treatment. The Institute reacted accordingly. In preparation for Mme. Sembrich's two days of teaching per week, a list of staff duties was drawn up, including a standing order at the florist for lilies-of-the-valley, to be placed atop her piano.

Conductor Fritz Reiner, who took on leadership of the Curtis Orchestra in 1931, works with composer Gian Carlo Menotti.

Among the faculty there were the feared and the more feared. At the upper end of the scale were the tall and lanky London-born cellist, Felix Salmond, who tossed blackboard erasers at cello bows in an attempt to improve tone, and the short, rotund Russian, Isabelle Vengerova, pupil of Leschetizky and onetime professor of piano at the Imperial Conservatory in St. Petersburg, whose sarcasm struck like bolts of lightning. Violinist Flesch, a cultivated gentleman of European manners, was insulted when students did not bow in his presence. He did not return the courtliness, however — when a pupil displeased him, he would shout, "Send him [or her] to Juilliard!" Those confronted with such verbal assaults were duly shaken. Most survived; a few exited.

Along with their unique temperaments, the faculty members brought highly individual teaching styles. Voice teacher and noted recitalist Emilio de Gogorza had a novel approach: He would spend a whole year on one song, explaining that if you could teach a student to sing one song correctly, the entire repertoire would follow. Not everyone agreed.

Then there was the dapper Frenchman Louis Bailly, who taught chamber music, but with a highly irregular system. Up on the podium where he presided, facing the string players, were little lamps lit with colored bulbs. These he would push at will, like a traffic cop.

Surrounded here by admiring students, harpist and composer Carlos Salzedo (fourth from right) taught at Curtis for almost four decades, imparting his comprehensive knowledge of the instrument and its repertoire.

Cellist Felix Salmond works with student Leonard Rose,
later a Curtis faculty member as well as an acclaimed soloist (1938).

The Institute, as depicted in a 1920s postcard.

When the red light went on, it meant "Stop." Green meant "Go." There was also a purple light facing the piano, and when that one was lit — to the embarrassment of the musician seated at the instrument — it signaled that, "The pianist is too loud."

Students were expected to perform at the school and to be present for performances by fellow students and faculty. Names were checked off at the door, and full attention demanded — if you were caught laughing, you'd end up in the dean's office. The concerts were rigidly structured, with students of a given teacher appearing on the same program. One evening all the Flesch violin students might perform and, another evening, the piano students of David Saperton.

The Common Room served as the venue for recitals and also as a rehearsal hall for the student orchestra. Performance activities were given a boost when, in December 1927, a small concert hall was inaugurated in the main building with a recital by Josef Hofmann. First named Casimir Hall in honor of the pianist's father, and later renamed Curtis Hall, it was designed by Philadelphia architect Horace Wells Sellers. Seating 250, the hall at first was intended strictly for internal use.

Entrance doors of wrought-iron, Italian Renaissance in style, led to the handsome room, whose interior walls of white mahogany were paneled up to the arched ceiling, with furniture finished to match this softly-toned wood. The two balconies flanking the hall featured elaborate Yellin wrought-iron grilles with center panels representing unicorns. One of the hall's prized possessions was a four-manual Aeolian pipe organ donated by Cyrus H. K. Curtis; when the room was dedicated he played the first selection.

Academic studies were included at Curtis from the beginning. Students of high-school age and younger studied with one teacher, who supervised all their academic work. Classes started at 8 a.m. and were held weekdays and Saturdays. Musical subjects ancillary

Ancient Instruments Put to New Use

The seal of The Curtis Institute of Music, which was designed by architect Edwin H. Fetterolf, makes use of a square-shaped Hebrew lyre, flanked on each side by an instrument of ancient Egypt known in Latin as sistrum, and in Egyptian as seshesh. The form of lyre depicted on the seal dates from the second century B.C., and sistra were found in the tomb of King Tutankhamen, who died c.1358 B.C.

to instrumental instruction included transcription, clef reading, score reading, eurythmics and platform deportment (with instructions on how to pick up a dropped handkerchief).

College-level students took courses in such subjects as psychology, literature and foreign languages, with faculty members drawn from major academic institutions, including the University of Pennsylvania. Eminent guests from Harvard and Princeton universities, Bryn Mawr College and major art museums presented lectures on the comparative arts. The renowned French pedagogue, composer and conductor Nadia Boulanger visited for a week, lecturing on "The Little Organ Book of Johann Sebastian Bach."

In the school's second academic year, Mrs. Bok turned her attention to the establishment of the Library, purchasing an excellent basic collection of books and musical scores. Soon a Victrola and a Duo-Art player piano, along with records and piano-rolls, were added. Special collections were developed of musical manuscripts, letters, early printed books and first editions. In 1930, Mrs. Bok bought the Burrell Collection of Wagneriana for the Library. At the time this was the most important set of unedited and unpublished documents in existence relating to composer Richard Wagner, encompassing more than five hundred items.

Aware of the importance of passing on the Curtis legacy in concrete form, the administration began to publish an internal newsletter, *Overtones*, in October 1929. Though for reasons of economy the publication was at times suspended, it was always revived; today's volumes form an invaluable source of information. And, from 1936 to 1940, recordings were made of performances aired on weekly radio broadcasts from Curtis, another important archival resource.

The Curtis Institute's first director, Johann Grolle, resigned in 1925 to return to his previous position as Head Worker of the Settlement Music School, at which time William E. Walter, a businessman with a background in music criticism and orchestra management, took over The Institute's leadership.

The Common Room in the mid-1920s.

The foyer of Knapp Hall in the early days.

Director Josef Hofmann, on right, with David Saperton, piano faculty member.

Chapter Two

The Hofmann Years

The Hofmann Years

A Visionary Leader

In 1927, The Curtis Institute of Music appointed its third director, a man who would remain at the helm for twelve years and who would play a crucial role in determining The Institute's long-term future. He was Mary Bok's partner in castle-building and head of the piano faculty, Josef Hofmann.

Mr. Hofmann's directorship gave the young conservatory enormous cachet in the musical world, helping to attract prestigious new faculty members and gifted students from an ever-broadening geographic base. His personal credo for The Curtis Institute of Music, one that was often echoed by Mary Bok, was: "To hand down through contemporary masters the great traditions of the past." To fulfill that goal, Mr. Hofmann wanted fewer students (at the time he took over, enrollment was reduced from almost 300 to 229), which would allow for more intensive one-on-one study with the given instructor. He also pointed out the need for good practice instruments in the homes where the students would live. Accordingly, The Institute was soon the owner of virtually every orchestral instrument, in addition to its raft of Steinway pianos. Mr. Hofmann advocated that students continue their studies in the summer with their designated teachers, wherever those teachers might be — the Val d'Aosta in Italy; Krakow, Poland; or Lake George, New York. He desired as well to launch graduates of professional caliber through American and European appearances, arranged by prominent managers. Mrs. Bok took on these projects as a personal expense.

Particularly significant was Josef Hofmann's attitude toward tuition. When he became director, the tuition fee of $500 per year was paid by a small fraction of students whose families could afford it. This was not to Mr. Hofmann's liking. "Why these tuition fees?" he asked Mrs. Bok, as reported by her later. "Practically no student of talent can pay them in full, if at all. What would you think of abolishing tuition altogether? Then students would know that only their work is of value here." Mrs. Bok was in total agreement. Thus, from the

From left: Mrs. Calvin Coolidge and her husband, the U.S. President, with Mary Louise Curtis Bok and her husband, Edward Bok, at the dedication of the Singing Tower in Florida (1929).

1928/29 academic year onward, tuition was abolished in favor of full scholarships for all students. The catalogue stated simply that: "Sole requirements for admission are that the student shall demonstrate a native gift for music, a special aptitude for a chosen instrument and personal characteristics that indicate the possibility of continuous further development."

In Mrs. Bok the new director found a ready and willing listener who would accede with pleasure to his requests. Her original endowment of $500,000 was increased in 1927 to a total of $12.5 million — in those years a huge sum. In 1932, the Curtis board created a foundation to administer the endowment.

"Prince" of the Podium

Leopold Stokowski was no figurehead at Curtis. Rather, he was a real — and committed — presence as head of orchestral studies. To be sure, his efforts were not entirely altruistic, for he wanted to insure the continued supremacy of his own Philadelphia Orchestra. How better to achieve that than by training the next generation of players? Indeed, shortly after the founding of The Curtis Institute, he wrote: "I have always dreamed of an ideal training method for our [the Philadelphia] orchestra — at last it is come — in the student orchestras of The Curtis Institute. I can develop completely trained young artists fully equipped for every school of symphony playing — an opportunity of the highest value to our orchestra."

Although multiple commitments drew Leopold Stokowski away from Curtis after three years, he set the stage with characteristic energy and purpose and maintained a firm guiding hand when others took over. The symbiotic relationship served both

The Perfect Reed

Of all the legendary musicians lured by Leopold Stokowski to the Philadelphia Orchestra, none had a greater impact than the French-born oboist Marcel Tabuteau. As principal player with the Philadelphia ensemble for thirty-nine years and a Curtis faculty member for twenty-seven, he was a consummate musician, his tone immediately recognizable for its suave and supple character, and his search to maximize the instrument's potential, unending.

Yet Mr. Tabuteau's influence extended beyond the oboe — indeed, beyond the entire woodwind family. At Curtis, where he taught individual students, wind classes and string ensembles, he was renowned for his approach to musical phrasing, having developed what former student and distinguished oboist Laila Storch has referred to as "an elaborate system of numbers...which he applied to ranges of intensity, continuity of rhythm and patterns of phrasing."

Marcel Tabuteau was a man of lively wit, with an endless store of anecdotes. Whatever he did, he did wholeheartedly, whether it was the making of an oboe reed, fishing for salmon or seeking a win at the gaming tables.

institutions well. What could be more inspiring for a student than to be learning, both in class and in orchestral readings, from some of the world's finest musicians? In turn, Mr. Stokowski quickly began to reap the rewards of his efforts. In 1930, he plucked twenty-two-year-old harpist Edna Phillips, fresh from Curtis graduation, for the ranks of his own ensemble: one of the first women in an American symphony orchestra. By that same year, twenty-seven former Curtis students had joined the Philadelphia Orchestra. Not only the "Fabulous Philadelphians" gained from this superb teaching; other major ensembles around the country did as well.

Leopold Stokowski conducted his first orchestra rehearsal at The Institute on November 14, 1924, in the Common Room. In addition to the students, the assembled group included townspeople who played as a hobby or avocation. It was subsequently decided to divide this group into senior and junior sections, according to the level of expertise. Both groups gathered on the same evening every week in two of the Curtis buildings, one in the Common Room and the other in Knapp Hall. Mr. Stokowski and his designated associate conductor, Michael Press, arrived at seven o'clock and conducted one of the orchestras for an hour; at eight they switched ensembles. To assist and encourage the students, members of the Philadelphia Orchestra were asked to sit alongside their pupils and play during rehearsals. Mr. Stokowski assigned the teaching of all instruments except for the strings to his own orchestra's principal players. The first scores received for rehearsal were of three Mozart symphonies.

Watching Leopold Stokowski at the helm of the young musicians was a revelation to those present. Not a sound or movement escaped his observation, and when he stopped the orchestra to explain a passage or request, "the proverbial pin drop would have sounded loudly," according to one spectator, The Institute's librarian. Over and over Mr. Stokowski practiced details and explained by example or anecdote. If a passage went badly, every player was required to perform the passage alone until the source of the problem was discovered. Mr. Stokowski had a chart of the ensemble at his stand so there was no way to remain anonymous. He also initiated his own version of musical chairs by changing the seating at will. Complacency was not a sentiment felt within these walls.

Yet Leopold Stokowski was not unkind. Pianist and composer Abram Chasins, who was on the early faculty, wrote that Mr. Stokowski "got his results through the intensity of his own dedication — by example, not preachment. He was only testy and impatient with a lack of attention or effort. Each rehearsal sustained his reputation for toughness, but he was toughest on himself in enforcing self-imposed standards of excellence." When the rehearsal was over, reported Mr. Chasins, Mr. Stokowski would sprint into the library to pore over scores and listen to the latest recordings.

Students, aged six to fourteen in the 1938/39 academic year, stand at the school's main entrance.
Left to right: Unidentified, Elliott Fisher, Nathan Goldstein, Seymour Lipkin, Gary Graffman, Bianca Polack, Diana Steiner, Rudolf Favaloro, Charles Libove, Hyman Bress, Robert Cornman, Margot Ros.

In the next academic year Thaddeus Rich replaced Mr. Press as associate conductor. A first public concert was held April 25, 1926, at the Penn Athletic Club in Center City Philadelphia, both Curtis orchestras having been combined into one group. Messrs. Stokowski and Rich alternated in conducting the sixty-four students plus twelve members of the Philadelphia Orchestra. The composers represented, through short works and excerpts, included Lalo, Weber, Bach, Beethoven, Saint-Saëns, Sibelius and Anton Rubinstein (the latter with teenage Curtis piano student and future artist of world repute, Shura Cherkassky, as soloist). The concert was broadcast on Philadelphia radio station WIP, the first time that Curtis was heard via this medium.

During the 1927/28 season, Mr. Rich was succeeded by the Polish-born Artur Rodzinski, assistant conductor of the Philadelphia Orchestra, who, like Mr. Stokowski, was a proponent of new works. On April 24, 1927, the Curtis Orchestra presented a second concert, this time in Philadelphia's Academy of Music, which again was broadcast on radio. The student ensemble, now enlarged to eighty-six players, was similarly augmented by a dozen musicians from the Philadelphia Orchestra. Mr. Stokowski pulled one of his trademark coups at this event, employing seven harps instead of the customary two in the *Prince Igor* dances of Borodin.

Mr. Rodzinski took complete charge of the ensemble in its fourth season, greatly enlarging its numbers and taking it to Carnegie Hall in New York City. Also initiated were several coast-to-coast radio broadcasts with the Columbia and National Broadcasting networks.

Yet another staff change occurred in 1929 when the Polish-born violinist/conductor/composer Emil Mlynarski was named conductor at Curtis. Mr. Mlynarski expanded the number of radio programs; in 1930, the orchestra was chosen to substitute for the New York

Lectures by such leading figures as music critic Samuel Chotzinoff added spice to the Curtis curriculum (1938).

Philharmonic in two regularly scheduled broadcasts. He also took the orchestra to Boston for a concert, the program including Richard Strauss' tone poem *Don Juan*.

An elderly and courteous individual, Emil Mlynarski, all agreed, was a very nice man. So nice, in fact, that under him the orchestra's discipline floundered significantly — people talked; they even played cards. The socializing wouldn't last long, for a tornado would soon arise in the form of Fritz Reiner, whom we shall meet shortly.

From Grand to Intimate: Opera and Chamber Music

Vocal study was from the beginning an integral part of the Curtis program and it quickly produced results. The first singer to be engaged by the Metropolitan Opera was Sembrich student Louise Lerch, who joined the New York company in 1926; in 1932, mezzo-soprano Rose Bampton began her long and illustrious association with the Met.

The first Curtis student production of opera took place on May 12, 1929, with a performance of Eugène d'Albert's *Tiefland* at the Academy of Music, Mr. Rodzinski conducting. That same year, The Institute affiliated with the Philadelphia Grand Opera Company, of which Mr. Stokowski was honorary music director, Mr. Mlynarski conductor, and Mrs. Bok principal patron and chairman of the board. Curtis students quickly began to participate in the stagings. During the first season alone twelve operas were presented, with seventeen Curtis opera students performing fifty-five roles; the student orchestra played in three of the operas.

Among many events of note, one production attracted banner headlines from coast to coast as well as the nation's most sophisticated audience of music lovers. This was the American premiere of Alban Berg's opera *Wozzeck*, on March 19, 1931, launched with a $40,000 start-up gift from Mrs. Bok. Mr. Stokowski conducted 116 members of the Philadelphia Orchestra, with twenty-five Curtis students supplying stage music in two scenes, and four vocal students — Abrasha Robofsky, Benjamin DeLoache, Albert Mahler and Edwina Eustis — appearing in the cast.

The conductor had demanded a remarkable number of rehearsals (eighty-eight preparatory, sixty on stage), and for six months Curtis was embroiled in the proceedings, with virtually all private lessons and classroom work diverted to some aspect of the opera. The initial rehearsals were taken over and singers coached by Sylvan Levin, a Curtis piano and conducting student who had come to Mr. Stokowski's attention and would form a long and loyal association with the maestro. Those not directly involved in the music were commandeered to design, build and paint scenery, make costumes, gather props and take on box office chores. Even the porters were put to work painting sets.

The performance was a huge success. Raved *Time* magazine, "While the Metropolitan [Opera] was lavishing its resources last week on the revival of Pietro Mascagni's sleazy *Iris*, the enterprising opera company which Mary Louise Curtis Bok finances in Philadelphia was absorbed in preparing for the most important U.S. premiere of the season (Berg's *Wozzeck*)."

Mr. Stokowski also gave the students an opportunity to perform with the Philadelphia Orchestra in his concert version of Mussorgsky's *Boris Godunov*. Natalie Bodanya, a Sembrich student, took on a minor role (Mr. Stokowski took a fancy to her and started to call her "Lollipop"), as did Ms. Bampton and Irra Petina. An April 1930 performance of Schoenberg's *Die Glückliche Hand*, given first in Philadelphia and later at the Metropolitan Opera House in New York, also featured Curtis students, as did the April 8, 1932, performance of Schoenberg's massive *Gurrelieder* on the stage of the Met with an augmented orchestra of 132, three male choruses, mixed chorus and five soloists, one being Ms. Bampton. That performance was recorded by RCA.

Soprano Margaret Daum, the original Amelia of alumnus Gian Carlo Menotti's opera Amelia Goes to the Ball, *poses with the composer and Mrs. Bok at the April 1937 premiere.*

Another major effort in the early years was a secular performance of the Gabriel Fauré *Requiem* for vocal soloists, chorus, organ and orchestra, presented April 19, 1931, at the Philadelphia Art Museum to an audience of 4,000; the conductor was Louis Bailly. The next year the *Requiem* was given again at Carnegie Hall, along with the first movement of the Tchaikovsky Piano Concerto in B-flat minor. The soloist in the latter work, then a student of Mr. Hofmann and David Saperton, was Cuban-born Jorge Bolet, who later was to become a renowned virtuoso, as well as head of the Curtis piano faculty.

Not all the instrumental performances at The Institute were monumental in size, for chamber music took its quiet place in 1927, when a student ensemble was born that for many years remained one of the school's greatest prides. Originally it was called the Swastika Quartet, after Mary Bok's estate in suburban Merion, which, in turn, had been named, at poet Rudyard Kipling's suggestion, for an ancient Indian symbol. However, with the rise of Nazism and the use of the swastika as party symbol — albeit with the arms differently aligned — the name became objectionable. In 1932, the ensemble was renamed the Curtis String Quartet, thus crediting the institution where it had originated.

The Quartet's original members were: first violinist Gama Gilbert, second violinist Benjamin Sharlip, violist Sheppard Lehnhoff and cellist Orlando Cole. Mr. Cole was the one musician to stay with the ensemble for its entire existence, though early on he was joined by Max Aronoff as violist and Jascha Brodsky as first violinist. The three played together for over half a century and served on the Curtis faculty as well. (The second violinist's position was held for a time by Mehli Mehta, father of conductor Zubin Mehta, and later by Yumi Ninomiya Scott, who has been on the faculty since 1970 and is a member of the Philadelphia Orchestra.)

From the beginning, the musicians played on school instruments, but hardly the workhorse variety that one might normally find at an academic institution. Rather, these were among the extraordinary gifts Mary Bok had made to The Institute: two Stradivarius violins, a Nicolò Amati viola and a Montagnana cello. So valuable were these instruments that the Quartet once housed them in a midwestern jail for safekeeping while they went to a movie. Unfortunately, a different officer was on duty by the time they returned, and the only way they could prove they were the rightful owners was by playing for him. On another occasion, Canadian officials wouldn't allow the Quartet in or out of the country without a check for the instruments' full value. Mr. Brodsky wrote a check for $100,000; at the time he had $40 in his account.

The Quartet was well received even in its earliest years, with local performances at the Ethical Culture Society and First Free Library, and with such offerings as the complete cycle of Beethoven string quartets. Chamber music concerts featuring the Curtis Quartet and other ensembles were put on by Louis Bailly at the Art Museum on Sunday evenings. Mr. Bailly, who had formerly been a member of the renowned Flonzaley Quartet, was attempting, in his own words, "to kindle a flame where none existed before," and in that he succeeded. People sat everywhere — on the balcony, on the steps, with the musicians on the landing of the main hall. At the end of the 1928/29 season of six concerts, it was reported that a total of 30,000 people had been in attendance — hardly the intimate gathering ideal for chamber music, but gratifying nonetheless.

Soon the Curtis String Quartet traveled to other major cities, including New York, Boston, Chicago and Washington, D.C., where, in 1934, the venue was the White House and the audience, President and Mrs. Franklin Delano Roosevelt. Happily, the public responded enthusiastically to even the more esoteric works in their repertoire. A major achievement was the ensemble's pioneering recordings for the Westminster label of the basic chamber music literature. The European-based company brought its equipment to a town in Connecticut and the Quartet sat down to record fourteen sides, each in one sitting, before a single microphone.

In 1935 the Quartet traveled to Europe, the first American-trained chamber group to tour that continent. The trip had been arranged by the English-Speaking Union in honor of King George's Silver Jubilee. That same year the ensemble recorded Curtis graduate Samuel Barber's haunting *Dover Beach* for string quartet and solo voice. The soloist was a fine baritone: Mr. Barber himself. In addition to his composition studies at Curtis with Mr. Scalero and the piano studies with Mme. Vengerova, the brilliant young musician had studied voice with Mr. de Gogorza.

The sponsor whose quietly given funds enabled this and other groups to exist and flourish was, of course, Mary Louise Curtis Bok.

SEPARATE CHECKS

ARTISTS ARE EXPECTED TO HAVE STRONG OPINIONS, BUT THREE CURTIS FACULTY MEMBERS BACK IN THE ERA OF JOSEF HOFMANN WERE MORE OPINIONATED THAN MOST. THEY ARGUED CONSTANTLY AT REHEARSALS ABOUT HOW SOMETHING WAS TO BE PLAYED, THEN WALKED ACROSS THE STREET TO THE DRUGSTORE WHERE THEY ORDERED NICKEL COKES AND SHOUTED IN UNISON, "SEPARATE CHECKS, PLEASE!"

Pianists and alumni/faculty members Eleanor and Vladimir ("Billy") Sokoloff.

Future Curtis president/director Gary Graffman at a lesson with Isabelle Vengerova (1938).

A Yellow-Haired, Pink-Ribboned Prodigy

Mrs. Bok's influence extended far beyond monetary generosity, beyond philosophical commitment. For in a scene of high stress and a student body of tender years, she was a warm and welcoming presence, somehow making the conservatory a family. She arrived at the school every day, simply but elegantly attired, emerging from a large maroon limousine with gold silk curtains at both rear side windows, her chauffeur wearing a matching uniform. She knew all the students by name, and they called her "Mother Bok" or "Aunt Mary." She sent them to a youth center for exercise and provided tickets to the Philadelphia Orchestra (sometimes they even got to sit in the conductor's box with illustrious guests). As her own personal life demanded less — by 1933, both her parents and her husband had died and her sons were married — her commitment to The Institute became ever greater.

A cherished and continuing Curtis tradition began in 1925 with the serving of tea every Wednesday afternoon at three o'clock. Students and faculty gathered in the Common Room, where Mrs. Bok and a chosen guest (sometimes the wife of a prominent conductor or composer) would pour. She also gave parties in her home for the entire school, often with concerts, and had picnics on the grounds. Concerned about the students' daily meals, she opened a cafeteria in The Institute, which was particularly welcome during the Depression. Here, home-cooked meals were prepared by a full-time cook. Soon the cafeteria was discovered by the faculty, at which point, according to a newspaper article, the hours of lunch and dinner formed a period "not scheduled in the Curtis catalogue, during which students and teachers fraternize over the coffee cups."

At the end of every school year Mrs. Bok addressed the student body, speaking extemporaneously and offering encouragement as well as tidbits of advice. Among the latter was a description of her ideal Curtis student: "no pose, no affectations of dress, hair or manner, no artistic temperament, no long hair."

At the annual holiday party, Mrs. Bok's strict dress code of ties and jackets for the boys and well-starched dresses for the girls was not only relaxed but overturned, for the performers, at least. Indeed, she paid for the outlandish costumes they wore in connection with the staged revues and skits. As described in an *Overtones* article from the 1932/33 academic year, the holiday party was the one occasion each year when "The Curtis Institute as a body lays aside its earnest demeanor, forgets its dignity and frolics like a spring lamb."

Even the music was of a different sort: the waltz, the Charleston and, a bit later, jitterbug. Everyone danced — including Mrs. Bok, who took a turn around the room with each student. Tables were piled high with food, Mme. Sembrich contributing thirty pounds of candy each year. The transformed dress code inspired faculty as well as students. One year

Cuba to the Rescue

When, in 1927, fifteen-year-old Cuban-born pianist Jorge Bolet was awarded a scholarship to study under Curtis Director Josef Hofmann, the question of providing for his living expenses was brought up. The Cuban government came to the rescue by voting an annual subsidy for the purpose.

Mrs. Bok was herself an accomplished pianist. Here, at the 1938 holiday party, she is applauded by alumnus/ faculty member Samuel Barber.

Carlos Salzedo disguised himself as the Phantom of the Opera. Another time a huge little girl with pink ribbons in her yellow hair, who had been introduced as a prodigy from "darkest Poland," toddled up to the stage and played — very badly, with lots of clinkers. Someone instructed her on how to play correctly, after which she offered a dazzling rendition of Chopin's *Polonaise Militaire*. Who was she? Josef Hofmann.

Then there was Gian Carlo Menotti's *Catalogue*, a mini-opera in which the irreverent young student composer, soon to be a major force on the musical scene, set the Curtis catalogue to music. It was not an easy feat to derive melody from such words as: "Students are on probation during the entire period of their enrollment," but the young Italian, who had first arrived in this country bearing a letter of recommendation from Mrs. Arturo Toscanini, managed it. No less clever were the skits presented by other students, which typically poked fun at Curtis teachers — clearly the only time they could get away with it.

When summer came, Curtis moved north. Between the end of the 1920s and World War II, Rockport, Maine — a scene of sea and rocky shores crowned with pine and white birch — became The Institute's informal summer home. Here, on the shore of Penobscot Bay, Mrs. Bok's parents had purchased a summer home, "Lyndonwood," as well as a next-door property which they gave to their daughter. When the Depression hit, Mrs. Bok purchased most of the land around the harbor and hired the unemployed to restore the deserted, rundown townhouses, which would become the focus of the Curtis summer music colony.

From this bucolic spot she played host to many of The Institute's faculty, as well as to other leading musicians from around the world. For favored faculty members she provided private housing, while students boarded in a community house with a member of The Institute staff in charge. Teachers mapped out a work program and performance schedule for the students. Eventually the Curtis String Quartet began to play in the nautical setting of Captain Eell's Boat Barn; on one occasion the ensemble performed with Elisabeth Schumann, one of the greatest interpreters of German lieder and a Curtis faculty member.

Maine was also home to the Harp Colony of America, begun in nearby Camden by Carlos Salzedo, which attracted musicians from around the world for study and performance. The French-trained harpist was one of the most important exponents of that instrument in its history. Not only did he compose and transcribe with impeccable taste, he also designed and supervised the construction of his own harp, which has become a model for contemporary instruments. In his Curtis association of nearly four decades, Mr. Salzedo taught some of the finest harpists to grace the stage. One of them, Alice Chalifoux, became first harpist of the Cleveland Orchestra and was his designated successor as head of the Camden colony.

There were always many guests at Rockport, including such maestri as Eugene Ormandy and Fritz Reiner, the latter arriving in the first sixteen-cylinder Cadillac anyone had ever seen. Student composers Menotti and Barber preferred sailing; on a calm day, passing boats would be treated to strains of opera sung by the two musicians, from *Carmen* to *Boris Godunov*.

Even Director Hofmann came to Rockport, having packed up all the equipment used in his hobby as an inventor and arriving with assistant in tow. On occasion, he too would give concerts. Admittedly, the entertainment in Rockport was not always terribly highbrow. Cellist Salmond, for instance, liked to belt out British barroom ballads, complete with a jig. Pierre Luboshutz, a pianist by trade but a stand-up comic by instinct, once conducted a choir of singers who faked their way through risqué Russian songs, while Mr. Luboshutz beat time on the floor with a broom handle. One night he did an Apache dance with cellist Gregor Piatigorsky (later a faculty member), who wore a maternity dress — the only outfit big enough for him.

It is hardly surprising that the warm and intimate Curtis ambiance, both at home and away from home, proved the catalyst for a number of romances. One of the first marriages to come out of The Institute — but surely not the last — was of piano students Eleanor Blum and Vladimir ("Billy") Sokoloff, both of whom graduated in 1938. Together the couple devoted six decades of their professional lives to Curtis — he as head of the concert division, coach and accompanist, playing over the years for thousands of student auditions, lessons and performances, and she as teacher of piano to generations of students, over seventy-five of whom have performed with the Philadelphia Orchestra.

"Play No More"

Henri Temianka, Scottish-born violinist of Polish parentage, who was among the first graduating artists of The Curtis Institute of Music, was a student in Berlin when he heard that the renowned violinist Carl Flesch was in the city. Young Temianka sought an audition with Mr. Flesch but did not even get to meet him. At a friend's urging, he persisted and succeeded in playing for the master. After finishing his first selection, there was silence, which Mr. Flesch finally broke by saying only: "Play no more."

The disheartened student prepared to depart, but then Mr. Flesch said: "I am leaving tomorrow for America. Go home and pack your bags — you are coming with me." A month later Henri Temianka was a Curtis student.

A First Commencement

Josef Hofmann had resisted the idea of formal commencement ceremonies because he wanted Curtis students to be known for their musical excellence, rather than as recipients of a scroll of achievement. Eventually, however, he capitulated. The first commencement exercises to be held at The Curtis Institute of Music took place on May 22, 1934, the tenth year of the school's existence. In all, over seventy participants were recognized, including thirty-four current graduating students and many who had previously earned their diplomas.

The doors of Casimir Hall swung open at 3:15 p.m. to admit the procession of graduates, speakers and officials. Carnations of red and white, the colors of The Institute, filled the stage. Mary Bok's hood bore the red and blue of the University of Pennsylvania, from which she had received honorary doctorates in both humane letters and music; the University was represented by its president, Dr. Thomas Sovereign Gates.

Flags of the United States and Poland were prominently displayed and both national anthems performed, in tribute to the school's Polish-born director, as well as Mary Bok's efforts to promote close ties with that nation, for which she had been decorated by the Polish government. (There were also close ties to Old Russia, with so many former Imperial Conservatory graduates enhancing the Curtis faculty roster that the school was jokingly referred to as the "St. Petersburg Conservatory-in-Exile.")

Awarded honorary degrees on this occasion were the pianist/composer Leopold Godowsky and Marcella Sembrich, who by then was retired and in delicate health. When she entered on the arm of Mr. Hofmann the audience rose as one and gave her prolonged applause. "How often," said the director, addressing her publicly, "I have sat entranced, listening to your golden voice, your interpretation noble and pure...."

After the formalities were over and the graduates had filed out to the organ strains of César Franck's *Grande Pièce Symphonique*, Casimir Hall became the scene for a reception and dancing. Then it was back to the business of music.

The Curtis Orchestra had been given a powerful boost with the arrival in 1931 of Fritz Reiner, who left the helm of the Cincinnati Orchestra to become conductor of the Philadelphia Grand Opera Company. (Mr. Reiner had hoped to succeed Leopold Stokowski as conductor of the Philadelphia Orchestra but lost that plum job to Eugene Ormandy.) During Mr. Reiner's ten-year association with Curtis, in addition to heading the student ensemble, he taught a small class of advanced conducting students and had responsibilities in the opera department. Under him, the Orchestra rehearsed, traveled to New York, Boston and Washington, D.C., and was heard in weekly broadcasts over the CBS radio network. Serving as Mr. Reiner's assistant conductor shortly after his own graduation from Curtis was Boris Goldovsky. The son of faculty member and violinist Lea Luboshutz, Mr. Goldovsky later earned an international reputation in the world of opera.

Fritz Reiner inspired respect — even terror. He was said to have a gimlet eye that could pierce victims like a dagger (even when he looked at them from the side). And he had a tongue to match. The simple German phrase *total unbegabt*, which means "completely untalented," could flatten the most inflated ego when uttered disdainfully in his Hungarian accent.

One of the world's master oboists, faculty member Marcel Tabuteau enjoyed a good smoke as much as he did a perfectly produced tone.

But he was a master, this man who wielded his baton with a tiny, precise beat. A superlative technician (albeit a conservative programmer), Mr. Reiner attracted exceptionally talented conducting students, demanding of them excellent sight-reading skills, a clear awareness of musical styles, and, in his own written words, "the ability to conduct an important work clearly and musically WITHOUT previous rehearsing with an orchestra."

During Fritz Reiner's tenure, Curtis undertook two full-scale productions of opera. The first was in 1935, when Rossini's *Il Barbiere di Siviglia* was presented, with Mr. Reiner on the podium and staging by Herbert Graf. The second was a major event both for the conservatory and the world of music: the April 1, 1937, world premiere of the opera *Amelia Goes to the Ball* by Gian Carlo Menotti, dedicated to Mary Bok. It was presented in a double bill with *Le Pauvre Matelot* by Darius Milhaud. A year later *Amelia* made it to the Met, launching the career of one of this century's most original and popular of operatic composers. Mr. Menotti, who had graduated from Curtis in 1933, remained a favorite of Mrs. Bok, and she continued to provide financial support for him — as she did for a number of other composers — long after he became world-renowned. So deep was her affection that she named her cocker spaniel Amelia.

Another significant event, which took place November 28, 1937, was Josef Hofmann's Golden Jubilee concert, held at the Metropolitan Opera House in New York, commemorating the pianist's American debut fifty years earlier. The Curtis instrumental faculty and many alumni had volunteered to join forces with the students in this concert, conducted by Mr. Reiner. Ending the program was a work entitled *Chromaticon*, for piano and orchestra, by one Michel Dvorsky, a suspiciously unknown composer. Almost everyone at the event, however, knew this to be a pseudonym for Josef Hofmann himself.

The renowned pianist resigned the next year from his directorship of Curtis. Who would succeed him? Times were very different, for although the school had made extraordinary strides during its short life, it was not immune to troubles outside its walls. The Great Depression had overtaken the country, and The Institute's endowment, which once had seemed enormous, was now recognized as insufficient to assure a long-term future.

In response to the growing crisis, drastic steps had been taken. Enrollment was reduced, some departments were reorganized and others eliminated, the school year was shortened, and salaries reduced. Madame Vengerova showed her loyalty by teaching for one year at no pay — just train fare and a hotel room on her weekly trip from New York City. Some wanted to close the school entirely and move to Maine. In terms of teaching philosophy, many felt that students should be more pragmatically educated; the so-called "star-breeding" system was not to their liking.

In this bleak and worrisome setting, a new type of leader was sought.

Conductor Fritz Reiner, seen here in a Napoleonic pose, inspired both respect and fear (1933).

Director Randall Thompson, a distinguished composer with strong academic credentials, works at the piano with students (1940).

Chapter Three

The Thompson Years

AN ACADEMICALLY-INCLINED LEADER

Composer Randall Thompson was appointed director of The Curtis Institute of Music in June 1939, remaining in that position for less than two years. A student of Ernest Bloch, he was educated at Harvard University and, prior to coming to Philadelphia, was professor of music at the University of California. Mr. Thompson had written a substantial number of orchestral works, an opera, a string quartet and piano music, but was best known for his choral music.

Having carried out a study of music education in U.S. colleges, Randall Thompson felt that a well-rounded, interdisciplinary background was essential for every Curtis student — more essential than virtuoso playing. To this end he inaugurated compulsory weekly assemblies featuring lectures and recitals. At the first of these he led the entire group in singing Bach chorales and works by Mozart and Palestrina. During Mr. Thompson's tenure a madrigal chorus was led by Samuel Barber, who by then had joined the faculty. Attention was given to performance and discussion of works written since the turn of the century through a "Twentieth-Century Group," whose advisers were Mr. Thompson and composer Aaron Copland.

Among the new faces in the Thompson years was pianist Rudolf Serkin. Born in Bohemia of Russian parents, Mr. Serkin had made his debut with the Vienna Symphony Orchestra at age twelve, rapidly developing an international career as recitalist, orchestral soloist and chamber musician. When he joined the Curtis faculty, Mr. Serkin was in his thirties and already recognized as one of his generation's most important musicians.

Two names stand out in the student roster during this period, not only for their remarkable careers, but for their friendship, forged at Curtis. They were Leonard Bernstein and Lukas Foss — musicians whose influence extended far beyond their own compositions, their appearances at the podium and at the piano. Mr. Bernstein brought music to vivid life for generations of Americans through his books and radio and television appearances, while Mr. Foss championed the integration of contemporary music into the traditional concert life.

Life at Curtis was not particularly happy for Leonard Bernstein, who had come to Philadelphia newly graduated from Harvard University. He greatly admired some of his teachers, notably Mme. Vengerova and Mr. Reiner, and he developed a friendship with Director Thompson, sharing in a mutual addiction to British crossword puzzles. Mr. Bernstein was also befriended by his adored solfège teacher, Renée Longy, who regularly fed him what he later referred to as "a French concoction of fried soup." But students found him arrogant — some even suspecting him of being a fake who pretended to read musical scores.

The nadir was reached with the formation of an "anti-Bernstein club" and a plot on the part of one unbalanced and jealous student to kill him, along with Messrs. Reiner and Thompson. Fortunately, the student tipped his hand and the deed was prevented. The unexpected result was that the student body rallied en masse to Mr. Bernstein's side, with fast friendships and shared musical experiences ensuing.

It was not until many years later that Mr. Bernstein, speaking at the school's fiftieth year celebration, revealed the sequence of events. He also explained that he had come to Curtis imbued with the humanistic values of Harvard at a time when Fascism and Nazism were threatening the free world. The Curtis Institute of Music seemed to him an alien land with an isolationist attitude, "an island of musical enterprise." He later came to realize the values and limits of each type of education. "Truth and beauty still form a valid equation," said Mr. Bernstein.

There may have been a shortage of money at Curtis in these last years before America's entry into World War II, but there was no shortage of performing talent on the part of students, graduates and faculty. Concerts continued in abundance. Elisabeth Schumann presented an evening of lieder. Rudolf Serkin and his violinist father-in-law, Adolf Busch, played sonatas. Carlos Salzedo conducted an ensemble of eight harps. Fortunately for Philadelphians not invited to attend such concerts, many of these events were heard over CBS Radio.

The flow of eminent guest composers and conductors continued as well during the Thompson years, including Sir Thomas Beecham, Georges Enesco and, once again, Nadia Boulanger. One special performance, in 1941, was the first U.S. production in English of the Debussy opera *Pelléas et Mélisande*, directed by Sylvan Levin of the Philadelphia Opera Company, with the orchestra made up in large part by Curtis students. The event was attended by a distinguished audience, including the work's librettist, Maurice Maeterlinck.

There were festive gatherings too, such as a holiday party at which actress Eva Le Gallienne gave a reading and Rose Bampton and Sam Barber sang — he with Mrs. Bok as accompanist. Among the visitors to Curtis were the Trapp Family Singers, newly escaped from a Europe that had erupted in war. They sang German choral music, danced their native ländler and did a yodel from the Austrian Alps. One wonders how heavy a presentiment lay over the assembled guests as to America's involvement in World War II.

Director Efrem Zimbalist and his wife, Mary Louise Curtis Bok Zimbalist, pose at the Settlement Music School. She had been a generous early supporter of the school, where her work led to the founding of The Curtis Institute of Music.

Chapter Four

The Zimbalist Years

A CHARMING ELF

Randall Thompson resigned from the directorship of The Curtis Institute of Music in 1941. The Board of Trustees had increasingly come to feel that The Institute would be best served by a return to its original mission: training the most gifted young musicians for performing careers at the highest level. The individual who succeeded Mr. Thompson was ideally suited to that purpose: Efrem Zimbalist, head of the violin faculty. Mr. Zimbalist remained in this position for twenty-seven years — the longest directorship to date.

A small, dapper man who liked good cigars, vintage wines, Chinese dressing gowns and poker games, "Zimmy," as he was affectionately known, was described more than once as a "charming elf." He delighted people with his old-world charm, his childlike enthusiasm, his skills as a raconteur. And he was generous; in the early years at Curtis he often treated the entire student body, along with their dates, to dinner after a recital.

Mr. Zimbalist's life was as colorful as his personality. Born in 1889 in the Ukrainian seaport Rostov-on-the-Don, he began to study with his violinist father at age six. At nine, he ran off to join an opera orchestra in the Caucasus, where he was found by his mother in the second concertmaster's seat, attired in short breeches. At twelve, he was a student of Leopold Auer at the Imperial Conservatory in St. Petersburg. After his celebrated Berlin debut using a Stradivarius violin borrowed from an admirer, Efrem Zimbalist went to England, where he remained five years. When he was twenty-two, Mr. Zimbalist moved to the United States, making his debut with the Boston Symphony Orchestra in 1911. His association with Curtis as a teacher of violin began in 1928, the same year that his own revered Leopold Auer joined the faculty as head of that department. With Mr. Auer's death in 1930, Mr. Zimbalist took his place.

The new director continued to teach at Curtis, inspiring students with his great love of music and the violin. He imposed upon them the same uncompromising standards that he demanded of himself (it was reported that he could easily practice one measure for four

Students study in the school library, which is now the Bok Room (1954).

Mrs. Zimbalist at her eightieth birthday celebration in Curtis Hall with Mrs. Eugene Ormandy (1956).

hours), but his manner with them was unfailingly polite. Mr. Zimbalist's criticisms were couched in such gentle language that, former students admitted, it sometimes took them a week to realize they'd been insulted.

Until 1950, Mr. Zimbalist also maintained an active schedule of concertizing. His tone was silken and seamlessly beautiful, his technique impeccable and his interpretations characterized by sincerity and restraint.

Audiences loved him. Whether in solo appearances with orchestras or in his annual Carnegie Hall recital, with loyal accompanist Vladimir Sokoloff by his side, Efrem Zimbalist always filled the house. (During the war years, Mr. Sokoloff temporarily transferred his loyalty to the U.S. Army. His place was taken by Jacob Lateiner, who at the time was a student of Isabelle Vengerova and who was released from school for this on-the-job training. Serkin student Seymour Lipkin was another young pianist who took on this challenge, accompanying Mr. Zimbalist on the violinist's 1944 tour of the U.S. and Canada.)

Efrem Zimbalist's taste in music was rather traditional. He particularly loved Brahms, was a passionate exponent of his fellow Slavs Rimsky-Korsakov and Glazunov, and, among contemporary composers, admired Richard Strauss and George Gershwin. On the whole, however, he felt that the music being written at that time suffered from a lack of repose and of heart.

Mr. Zimbalist was as well an occasional composer and conductor. Eugene Ormandy once stepped down from the podium at a Philadelphia Orchestra concert so that the violinist could conduct his own *American Rhapsody*. This and his other works were of the Romantic school, and he wrote in a variety of genres, from the tone poem to operetta.

As one of the first western musicians to perform in Asia, Efrem Zimbalist was immensely popular in that part of the world. The emergence of young virtuoso string players in Japan, Korea and China — not to mention the large numbers who eventually made their way to The Curtis Institute — was due in no small measure to Mr. Zimbalist and the few western artists who followed him.

When he took on the Curtis directorship, Efrem Zimbalist was widowed. His late wife had been the great American soprano Alma Gluck, by whom he had two children, a son and a daughter. Son Efrem Zimbalist, Jr., studied violin and composition and worked briefly as part of the Curtis administration, but found his niche as an actor, particularly on television, where he starred in *77 Sunset Strip* and *The FBI*.

On July 7, 1943, a front-page story appeared in *The Philadelphia Inquirer*, announcing that the previous day, Curtis Director Zimbalist had married Curtis founder Bok in a quiet family ceremony at the bride's summer home in Rockport, Maine. The marriage of the sixty-six-year-old widow and the fifty-four-year-old widower came as a surprise to all but their families and a few intimates. Even the close-knit Rockport community had no advance

A Day in Music History

On November 14, 1943, Leonard Bernstein, twenty-five-year-old pianist, composer and assistant conductor of the New York Philharmonic — not to mention a Curtis alumnus — took the helm of the New York ensemble after the briefest of notice, conquering the city and garnering front-page headlines across the nation.

Guest conductor Bruno Walter had developed the flu, and the Philharmonic's music director Artur Rodzinski was away on vacation, so Mr. Bernstein, who previously had led the ensemble only twice in rehearsal, was placed on call. He stayed up almost all night before the afternoon concert studying scores, then conducted the full program that included works by Schumann, Wagner, Richard Strauss and Miklos Rosza. The performance was broadcast nationally. Mr. Rodzinski motored down from the Berkshires to see his protégé, arriving at intermission. He agreed that Leonard Bernstein had done a wonderful job. "After all, I chose him for my assistant, didn't I?" he said.

notice. "Mother Bok" was now "Mother Zimbalist." Her presence at the school was still felt at Wednesday teas, recitals and graduations.

Cutting Back to Assure a Future

The challenges faced by The Curtis Institute of Music in the early 1940s were great, for the nation was in the wake of the Great Depression and on the verge of entering World War II. At home, the fortunes of the Curtis Publishing Company had plummeted, with the result that the school's endowment fell from $12.5 million to about half that.

Efrem and Mary Zimbalist responded to the crisis surrounding them by doing all in their power to salvage the school. She sold some of her Maine properties. He, assisted by the school's famously efficient treasurer and comptroller, J. H. Mattis, and his own stockbroker, succeeded in restoring the bulk of the lost endowment through wise financial moves. He also undertook to sell the school's many valuable musical instruments. Even one of the buildings went, Knapp Hall being sold to the Elizabeth Arden Sales Corporation in 1943. (Six years later, on January 20, 1949, a fire broke out in the third floor wall of the former Sibley house when a blowtorch ignited insulation in a third floor wall; fortunately there were no injuries, nor were any valuable musical holdings destroyed.)

Program cutbacks were initiated by Director Zimbalist in virtually all areas: the orchestra, opera, conducting, music theory and most instruments. Lacking the requisite financial support, the Curtis String Quartet departed Curtis, becoming the resident ensemble of the newly formed New School of Music on Pine Street in Philadelphia, whose director was Max Aronoff. Yet the ensemble retained the proud Curtis name, and its three longtime members — Mr. Aronoff, Orlando Cole and Jascha Brodsky — rejoined the Curtis faculty in the 1950s. The priceless instruments used by the Quartet were among those sold, replaced by an excellent set of copies made by William Moennig, Sr., in Philadelphia.

Given that many of the students and a few among the faculty were departing for military duty, the Zimbalists felt that a significantly decreased enrollment was not only to be expected but, in view of the financial constraints, was desirable. They also wanted to offer a more intensive ratio of faculty to students. When Efrem Zimbalist became director, enrollment stood at 173; in the height of the war years it was reduced to one hundred, then slowly zigzagged its way back up. The faculty was not exempt from cuts; many contracts were not renewed, and some people resigned.

Newspaper reports about Curtis now referred as much to war service as to music. Director Zimbalist's son, Efrem, Jr., an infantryman, was wounded, having stepped on a booby trap in Germany; he was sent to England to convalesce. Hans Wohlmuth, Viennese-born stage director and head of the Curtis opera department, completed an intensive course in mechanics and applied for work as a machinist, in loyalty to his adopted country. And Samuel Barber was inducted into the Army Air Force. Happily, the military saw fit to use his great talent, commissioning the thirty-four-year-old composer's second symphony, which made use of a specially constructed "tone generator" that simulated the sound of a radio beam. The work was premiered by the Boston Symphony Orchestra in 1944 and broadcast over short-wave radio. Corporal Barber was present in uniform to acknowledge the long applause.

Two other Curtis alumni were represented the same year in a performance of much emotional significance, when the world premiere was given in London of Marc Blitzstein's *Freedom Morning*, with Hugo Weisgall conducting. The symphonic poem was dedicated to the African-American troops in the U.S. Army. Its London performance and a later one by the Philadelphia Orchestra drew international attention.

What is remarkable is that in these difficult times The Curtis Institute of Music survived and even flourished — albeit in a more modest guise. Ironically, Curtis continued to have an image of perpetual wealth, deriving from the affluence of its origins. That false impression was abetted by the fact that The Institute became increasingly cut off from the outside world, its daily concerts, now held at 5:15 in the evening, open only to the Curtis family (except by special invitation), its doings private.

Two musical giants converse: pianist Mieczyslaw Horszowski, on left, and cellist Pablo Casals. Both were active musicians to the end of their lives, Mr. Horszowski passing the one-hundred year mark and Mr. Casals, ninety-six (1955).

KYW radio broadcast April 22, 1945: The Curtis Orchestra,
plus six members of the Philadelphia Orchestra, led by faculty member Marcel Tabuteau.

Faces Old and New

Important new faculty appointments were made during the Zimbalist regime, drawn in part by the magic of his name. Among these was Mieczyslaw Horszowski, a pianist and chamber musician of peerless integrity and luminous warmth, who became a member of the Curtis faculty in 1942 at age fifty, teaching until his death a half century later. A child prodigy who had attracted the interest of composers Ravel and Szymanowski, the pianist studied in Vienna with Theodor Leschetizky, teacher of Paderewski, Schnabel and Vengerova. He made his debut in that city at age eight and began to tour Europe and then the U.S. Among his greatest successes was a series of twelve recitals in New York's Town Hall where he presented Beethoven's complete works for solo piano, and a series of ten recitals of Mozart's piano music.

A tiny, self-effacing individual with twinkling eyes and a cherubic smile, Mr. Horszowski was loved and respected by his students and admired from a respectful distance by music lovers who observed him taking daily walks near his Rittenhouse Square abode, attired in his signature beret. Indeed, Philadelphia became so much Mieczyslaw Horszowski's home that New York felt shortchanged. "I do wish he would come over from Philadelphia a little oftener," sighed composer/critic Virgil Thomson after one of the rare Manhattan concerts.

Joining the violin faculty in 1944 was Ivan Galamian, born in Persia of Russian parents. The gentle man but stern teacher had developed a highly-regarded method of violin playing and teaching, which he distilled into a 116-page book. Despite such concrete assistance, the source of Mr. Galamian's magic as a teacher remained elusive, being as much a part of his soul as of his methodology. Also new to the faculty was violinist Veda Reynolds, who worked with Curtis string players during her tenure of almost two decades.

The viola, that much maligned "supporting" instrument, was given the stature it deserved with the arrival in 1942 of Scottish artist William Primrose, dubbed the "virtuoso violist," who was a gifted chamber musician as well. Mr. Primrose loved Philadelphia and proudly used an instrument made in that city by William Moennig, Jr., which he claimed to prefer over his three-centuries-old Antonio Amati viola.

Several faculty members of long tenure retired during the Zimbalist years. In the cello department, Felix Salmond left in 1943, his place taken briefly by Emanuel Feuermann, whose stellar career was cut short by his death at age thirty-nine. Mr. Feuermann was succeeded by Gregor Piatigorsky. The former first cellist of the Imperial Opera in Moscow had fled the Russian Revolution; legend has it that at one point he was forced to swim the Dnieper River, floating his cello ahead of him. The tall (6'3"), dark and handsome musician subsequently occupied the first desk of the Berlin Philharmonic. A Curtis faculty member for nine years,

Mr. Piatigorsky was a frequent, generous and usually anonymous donor to other musicians, lending money through third persons so that his colleagues and students could buy fine instruments — often without repayment. He gave many concerts while at Curtis, often accompanied by alumnus/faculty member Ralph Berkowitz.

Mr. Piatigorsky was succeeded in 1951 by Leonard Rose, principal cellist of the Cleveland Orchestra, who had been an assistant to Felix Salmond after graduating from Curtis; later he was also a member of the acclaimed Istomin-Stern-Rose Trio as well as an important soloist. In 1953, Orlando Cole of the Curtis String Quartet rejoined the faculty; he continues to teach today, a cherished link between Curtis past and present.

Harpist Carlos Salzedo, who died during the Zimbalist years, was succeeded in 1961 by Marilyn Costello, a Curtis graduate and principal of the Philadelphia Orchestra who taught at The Institute until her death in 1998. Composition suffered a loss with the retirement of Rosario Scalero, but fortunately Gian Carlo Menotti had joined the faculty, and in 1947 he was joined by George Rochberg, who had survived a World War II wound to enroll as a Curtis student several years before. Mr. Rochberg's distinguished oeuvre, comprising orchestral and chamber music as well as works for solo voice and orchestra, is notable for its dramatic shift from a highly individual form of serialism to tonality.

Before Rosario Scalero's departure, a future Pulitzer Prize winner had a last opportunity to study with him. George Walker of the class of 1945 had come to Curtis to study piano with Rudolf Serkin, but became intrigued with composition and applied to enter Mr. Scalero's class, graduating in both areas of study. Mr. Walker was one of the first African-Americans to graduate from Curtis. (A much earlier alumnus, J. Russell Johnson, who was in the class of 1928, helped to found the National Association of Negro Musicians.) At the end of George Walker's four years at Curtis, Mary and Efrem Zimbalist presented him in a piano recital at Town Hall in New York. The twenty-three-year-old bravely wedged three of his own pieces in between Schumann and Chopin. Guggenheim and Rockefeller fellowships followed, as did over seventy-five published works for orchestra, chamber ensembles, solo instruments and voice.

Another Pulitzer recipient who studied at Curtis with Mr. Scalero and later joined the faculty is Ned Rorem. However, their relationship was brief and unrewarding. Mr. Rorem recalled endless counterpoint lessons that resulted in his decision to avoid all emphasis on that craft with his own students. "A teacher of composers," he wrote in his autobiography, *Knowing When to Stop*, "must himself be a composer, one who has often heard his own works well played, and thus has the practical sound in his veins...."

Nevertheless, former students of Mr. Scalero continued to garner awards and commissions during the Zimbalist period. Samuel Barber's first opera, *Vanessa*, with libretto by

Gian Carlo Menotti, was produced at the Metropolitan Opera in 1958, and in 1966 Mr. Barber's *Antony and Cleopatra* opened the first Met season in its new Lincoln Center home. Mr. Menotti continued his own meteoric rise as an opera composer with *The Medium*, *The Telephone*, *Amahl and the Night Visitors*, *The Consul* and *The Saint of Bleecker Street*.

In the realm of conducting, the date of November 14, 1943, will stand forever in music history, for it was then that twenty-five-year-old Leonard Bernstein, assistant conductor of the New York Philharmonic, stepped in at the last minute for the ailing Bruno Walter and, overnight, became one of the world's best known classical musicians. He would take over the music directorship of the same ensemble fifteen years later.

A number of Curtis-trained instrumentalists also began to make their mark in the musical world. Among them was pianist Gary Graffman, a New York native of Russian background whose violinist father had been yet another Auer student. The precocious young musician was accepted at Curtis at the age of seven to study with Isabelle Vengerova; he auditioned carrying his own pedal extension to compensate for his short legs. Ten years later, in 1946, he graduated.

At eighteen, Mr. Graffman won the Philadelphia regional auditions in a piano contest sponsored by the Rachmaninoff Fund, Inc., and was engaged to play with the Philadelphia Orchestra under Eugene Ormandy. At twenty, he won the esteemed Leventritt Award (following in the footsteps of fellow Curtis alumni Sidney Foster and Eugene Istomin, who had won the Leventritt several years earlier). A solo appearance with the New York Philharmonic, which came with the award, was a major step in a career that would bring Gary Graffman international renown as a performing artist.

Other Curtis students and graduates were honored throughout the Zimbalist directorship. At the glamorous National Rachmaninoff Competition held at Carnegie Hall, Seymour Lipkin defeated Regional Laureate Graffman, winning the national award and playing with virtually every major American orchestra as a result. Canadian cellist Lorne Munroe received the Walter W. Naumburg Foundation Award, as did pianists Abba Bogin, Jorge Bolet, Abbey Simon and Zadel Skolovsky, and tenor Wayne Conner. Jaime Laredo, the brilliant young Bolivian-born violinist, missed his 1959 commencement because he was winning first prize in the illustrious Queen Elisabeth of Belgium Competition in Brussels. The 1950s boasted two more Leventritt winners: pianist Anton Kuerti and violinist Arnold Steinhardt.

In 1962, the year after her graduation, pianist Susan Starr was silver medalist in the Moscow Tchaikovsky Competition. (By then she was a veteran, having made her debut with the Philadelphia Orchestra fourteen years before, at age six.) Pianist Richard Goode, a 1964 graduate, won a Young Concert Artists Award while a student of Rudolf Serkin at Curtis;

MUSIC AND MORALE

STATEMENT BY MARY LOUISE CURTIS BOK, AT THE TIME OF WORLD WAR II:

"I BELIEVE WITH ALL MY HEART IN THE IMPORTANCE OF MUSIC AS A FORCE FOR MAINTAINING OUR NATIONAL MORALE, EVEN UNDER CONDITIONS OF WAR. A NATION THAT WOULD NOT MARCH TO MUSIC, OR COULD NOT SING, WOULD BE LACKING A VERY NECESSARY IMPETUS TOWARD DEFENSE. SPIRITUALLY, EVERY AMERICAN NEEDS THE INSPIRATION THAT MUSIC BRINGS."

Mr. and Mrs. Zimbalist at the annual Curtis holiday party in 1951.

he was to become one of the world's leading interpreters of Beethoven. In the same period, another Serkin, Peter, graduated from Curtis and began his own piano career. Rudolf Serkin's son would do great honor to the family name.

An Orchestra Reborn

The dynamic head of the Curtis Orchestra and conducting department, Fritz Reiner, had resigned in 1941 due to increasing responsibilities as music director of the Pittsburgh Symphony Orchestra. Alexander Hilsberg, longtime violin faculty member, who was concertmaster and assistant conductor of the Philadelphia Orchestra, was named to replace him. However, the Curtis Orchestra was disbanded in the 1942/43 season because so many students were called up for service in World War II, and did not regroup until 1947, when Mr. Hilsberg once again picked up the baton.

In the meantime, the instrumental faculty that would help to recreate the Orchestra was once again being built up. Mason Jones, principal horn of the Philadelphia Orchestra and a Curtis alumnus, returned to his alma mater to teach in 1946. Just as his teacher, Anton Horner, had created a dynasty of horn players to staff major American orchestras, so Mr. Jones did the same in his long Curtis career. He was a founder-member of the Philadelphia Brass Ensemble, whose members were mainly Curtis-connected; its recordings of the brass repertoire became famous.

In 1950, the Philadelphia Woodwind Quintet was formed by four Curtis alumni (Burnett Atkinson, flute; John de Lancie, oboe; Anthony Gigliotti, clarinet; Mason Jones, horn) and bassoonist Sol Schoenbach, who later became executive director of the Settlement Music School. The ensemble gave yearly concerts in Curtis Hall and made many recordings that became collectors' items. Flutist Murray Panitz, who was Mr. Kincaid's successor at the Philadelphia Orchestra, later served in the Quintet, along with Mr. Schoenbach's successor, Bernard Garfield. They, together with Messrs. de Lancie, Gigliotti and Schoenbach, all principal players in the Orchestra, brought the wind department into prominence at Curtis through their teaching. Student after student moved immediately from graduation to a major orchestra — including Philadelphia's own — sometimes in the first-desk position.

By 1949 the Curtis Orchestra was ready for a gala twenty-fifth anniversary celebration, held two nights running at the Academy of Music. On January 5, Alexander Hilsberg conducted the students in a program that included the overture to Berlioz's *Roman Carnival*, the local premiere of Barber's Symphony No. 2 and the Brahms Double Concerto

From left, Philadelphia Orchestra conductor and later a Curtis faculty member Eugene Ormandy, alumnus Gian Carlo Menotti and director Efrem Zimbalist, preparing for the 1952 world premiere of Menotti's violin concerto.

in A minor for Violin and Cello, with soloists Efrem Zimbalist and Gregor Piatigorsky. The student ensemble was augmented by two dozen members of the Philadelphia Orchestra. A congratulatory message appeared in the program book of the Philadelphia Orchestra, which noted that: "Its [the Curtis ensemble's] influence on the Philadelphia Orchestra has been almost incalculable; in fact, if all the Curtis alumni and alumnae were removed, the Orchestra would shrink to less than half its normal size."

The next evening, the opera department, with Efrem Zimbalist at the podium, presented *L'Oracolo* by Franco Leoni, sung in Italian; the "Letter Scene" from *Eugene Onegin* by Tchaikovsky, in Russian; and Gian Carlo Menotti's *Amelia Goes to the Ball*, in English. Baritone Frank Guarrera, a recent Curtis graduate and new member of the Metropolitan Opera, earned critical praise in the leading role of *L'Oracolo*, as the proprietor of an opium den. Even these major performances at the Academy of Music were not open to the public; admission was by invitation only, to the city's musical elite.

In 1953, Mr. Hilsberg was succeeded as head of the Curtis Orchestra by William Smith, the new associate conductor of the Philadelphia Orchestra. Mr. Smith became a leading figure in music education, both at Curtis and the Philadelphia Orchestra, over a four-decade span, and the ties between the two institutions remained strong. Mary Zimbalist maintained a close personal association with the Philadelphia Orchestra, presenting a fine new organ to the Academy of Music in memory of her father; it was constructed by the Aeolian-Skinner company in 1960.

Opera was given a boost in 1950 when Herbert Graf, stage director for the Metropolitan Opera, became head of the Curtis opera department, remaining for a decade. Studying at Curtis during this period was Anna Moffo, student of Euphemia Giannini Gregory. Ms. Moffo also went on to the Met, achieving great success in the lyric/coloratura repertoire.

Alexander Hilsberg, concertmaster and associate conductor of the Philadelphia Orchestra, with faculty members Gregor Piatigorsky and Efrem Zimbalist.

Efrem Zimbalist, Jr. addresses the audience in Curtis Hall at a tribute concert for his father in April 1978.

Among Mr. Graf's productions was a 1958 staging of Puccini's one-act operas *Gianni Schicchi* and *Suor Angelica*. Bringing a poignant fragility to the role of Sister Angelica was California-born Benita Valente, a student of Martial Singher, former Metropolitan Opera baritone who headed voice at Curtis between 1955 and 1968. Ms. Valente is one of the most respected vocal artists of our time in opera, chamber music, oratorio and art song.

In 1956 Mr. Graf staged the opera *Landara*, by Curtis Director Zimbalist, who had composed it in honor of his wife's eightieth birthday. Given two performances at the Academy of Music, the opera featured students Ilona Kombrink and Wayne Conner and was conducted by Mr. Zimbalist. Everyone agreed that *Landara* wouldn't make the Met, but Mary Zimbalist loved the fanciful work set in a mythical South Sea island with its own princess.

That same year, a second concert honoring Curtis' founder was held, with Rudolf Serkin as pianist and Eugene Ormandy conducting the Curtis Orchestra. The two men, who were friends as well as colleagues, would later, during Mr. Serkin's tenure as Curtis director, bring the Philadelphia and the Curtis orchestras even closer.

On Herbert Graf's departure from Curtis, Mr. Singher became head of the opera department, inaugurating the practice of presenting scenes and acts from the standard repertoire. Among the works he staged were Mozart's *Così Fan Tutte*, Rossini's *Il Barbiere di Siviglia* and Puccini's *La Bohème*.

Chamber music did not have the great emphasis during the Zimbalist regime that it attained later, in part because the feeling at the time — notably among managers — was that musicians who devoted themselves to that form would not be taken seriously as soloists. Mr. Zimbalist was not himself a passionate advocate of chamber music, tending to look upon it as something one did in retirement. Yet many students participated in ensembles under the guidance of Mr. Primrose, who took Louis Bailly's place as chamber music coach in 1942, and who was later succeeded by his own student, Karen Tuttle. Jascha Brodsky, who had departed during the war years, returned in 1955 to teach violin and coach chamber music.

In 1964 a major chamber music group was born in the foothills of Vermont. This was the Guarneri String Quartet. Three of its four members were Curtis alumni who had often played together while at the school and who later joined the faculty. They were violinists Arnold Steinhardt and John Dalley, and violist Michael Tree, originally a violinist. (Mr. Zimbalist never quite recovered from Mr. Tree's switch to this "lesser" instrument — William Primrose's virtuosity notwithstanding.) The three met up with cellist David Soyer, a Philadelphian, as well as a future Curtis faculty member, in the Marlboro, Vermont, center for chamber music that, under Rudolf Serkin's leadership, would forge close ties with Curtis.

Mme. Euphemia Gregory and her student Anna Moffo at the Curtis holiday party in 1952.

Here, at the urging of Alexander and Mischa Schneider of the Budapest Quartet, as well as Mr. Serkin and Pablo Casals, they were encouraged to join forces.

The Guarneri members had to wait a year for Arnold Steinhardt to complete his obligations as assistant concertmaster of the Cleveland Orchestra, but during the wait the musical world was abuzz about the ensemble-to-be. Aware of this, Mischa Schneider joked: "Don't play a note! You'll ruin your reputation." But the advance notice was modest compared to the accolades that followed the Guarneri's New York debut in 1965.

Today the quartet is now well into its fourth decade, recognized as one of the world's greatest chamber ensembles. Remarkably, it still exists with its original four members, a record neither matched nor even approached by any other current chamber group.

Farewell to a Legend

Efrem Zimbalist retired from Curtis in 1968. His last day, he told his close friend Vladimir Sokoloff, was one of the saddest of his life. The twenty-seven years of his directorship and the thirteen preceding as faculty member had encompassed the best and the worst of times in our nation and in his beloved Curtis Institute of Music.

Mr. Zimbalist's wife and Institute founder, Mary Louise Curtis Bok Zimbalist, was now ninety-two years of age and in failing health. Mr. Zimbalist would remain with her in Philadelphia until her death in 1970, at which time he moved to Reno, Nevada, to be near his daughter, Maria Zimbalist Bennett. Although he suffered through more than one serious illness, Mr. Zimbalist remained his alert, cheerful self during most of his long life of ninety-six years, smoking six cigars and practicing one hour every day.

For his ninetieth birthday in 1978, the great violinist was able to make it back from Reno to Curtis, where a big celebration took place. Many of the former director's colleagues and students hadn't seen him since he left Philadelphia, and they gathered together to dedicate his former studio as the Efrem Zimbalist Room. A gala dinner and two concerts were held, featuring Mr. Zimbalist's music. Composers Gian Carlo Menotti, Samuel Barber and George Rochberg were in attendance, as were the Guarneri Quartet, pianist Jorge Bolet and even the great-grandson of Richard Wagner, Gottfried.

And, in recognition of Efrem Zimbalist's early trips to Asia, where he brought the gift of Western music, Curtis graduates Toshiya Eto and his wife, Angela Nudo, both violinists, flew in from Tokyo. Mr. Eto performed with their son, Michael, a pianist who, not surprisingly, was also a Curtis graduate.

It was, as they say, all in the family.

Farewell by a Master

Three thousand admirers filled New York's Carnegie Hall on November 14, 1949, when Efrem Zimbalist gave his farewell recital. The instant he played the first six notes of the Beethoven C minor Violin and Piano Sonata, wrote "New York Times" critic Olin Downes, "one knew that he was in the presence of a consummate musician, unsurpassed among violinists for the sincerity, the knowledge and the reverence in which he holds his art." After the formal program, the outpouring of affection, and, finally, the encores, Mr. Zimbalist walked off for a final time. The audience, wrote Mr. Downes, "was loath to let him go."

Director Rudolf Serkin.

Chapter Five

The Serkin Years

A TITAN OF THE KEYBOARD

The sixth director of The Curtis Institute of Music, like Josef Hofmann and Efrem Zimbalist before him, was a performing musician of international stature. Rudolf Serkin, one of the most important and revered artists of the twentieth century, was appointed director of The Institute in 1968. Also like his two predecessors, he was already an integral part of the Curtis family, having headed the piano faculty since 1939.

The Bohemian-born musician came from a poor family, his father an opera singer-turned-unsuccessful-businessman, who had gone bankrupt four times. Introduced into the salon of a patroness, the younger Serkin proceeded to Vienna, where he studied piano, making his debut with the Vienna Symphony in 1915 at the age of twelve. He also studied composition with Arnold Schoenberg, who remained a major artistic influence in his life despite a subsequent rupture in their relationship. In 1920 Mr. Serkin met violinist Adolf Busch, his future father-in-law, under whose aegis the young musician gave a Berlin performance attended by such luminaries as Artur Schnabel and Albert Einstein. The Serkin and Busch families settled in Basel, Switzerland, in 1927.

Rudolf Serkin's first United States appearance was in 1933 with the Busch Quartet at the Library of Congress in Washington, D.C. This was followed in 1936 by a New York debut as soloist with Arturo Toscanini and the New York Philharmonic. From then on he toured the U.S. annually. A regular participant in the Casals Festival in France and Puerto Rico, Mr. Serkin credited its founder, the great Spanish cellist Pablo Casals, as being another key influence in his life.

Rudolf Serkin's playing was characterized by a consuming intensity that charged every note with meaning but never veered into sentimentality. He paid scrupulous attention to structural and interpretive detail, and was constantly discovering new things in frequently-played masterpieces (notably, those of Beethoven and Schubert). Above all, listeners responded to the honesty of his approach. "From the beginning," wrote *New York Times* critic Harold Schonberg, "Serkin has never hit a note that was aesthetically false." In chamber music, one of his greatest loves, his piano melted into the ensemble.

Described as looking like a benign and slightly befuddled chemistry professor, Rudolf Serkin had a gentle and unpretentious nature. His friendly manner and expansive smile endeared him to students, and his well-developed prankster's streak emboldened them to treat the tall, lanky figure in rumpled clothes like a favorite grandfather — except, that is, when he was teaching them or performing. At the school, and in the outside world, Mr. Serkin had a reputation for knowing everything about music. When faced with specific problems or questions, other musicians often ended up saying, "Let's ask Rudi." His answers seemed to satisfy everyone — a trait that would stand him in good stead as director of Curtis.

While in that role, Director Serkin maintained an active career as a soloist, using his worldwide tours as opportunities to listen to hopeful young pianists who wished to attend Curtis. Among those accepted to study during his tenure as director were several who would later develop major careers, including Yefim Bronfman, Cecile Licad, André-Michel Schub and the late Steven De Groote. These musicians joined a long list of eminent pianists who, during Mr. Serkin's previous three decades as Curtis faculty member, had also studied under him.

One of the new director's major achievements was the strengthening of The Institute's relationship with the Philadelphia Orchestra. Key to that success were his own appearances with the professional ensemble and his friendship with its music director, Eugene Ormandy. This dated from Mr. Serkin's arrival in the U.S., when Hungarian émigré Ormandy claimed to have given Mr. Serkin a lesson in tipping, American-style. Gradually, the two became close: Mr. Ormandy, the outgoing personality, and Mr. Serkin, the shy and somewhat reticent presence.

Director Rudolf Serkin, on left, with faculty member Felix Galimir. The two shared a deep love of chamber music and emphasized its study at Curtis.

The great warmth between Mr. Serkin and the Philadelphia Orchestra was demonstrated in 1951, at a special concert benefiting the orchestra's maintenance fund. After playing not one but three concertos in the one evening, Mr. Serkin was presented on stage with a bright red tractor for his Vermont farm. In his full dress of white tie and tails, the delighted soloist climbed up on its seat, his three-year-old son and future pianist, Peter, by his side.

Upon taking on the Curtis directorship, Mr. Serkin invited Eugene Ormandy to join the faculty, conducting the school's orchestra and supervising its training program. This Mr. Ormandy did, spending many Saturday mornings at The Institute in readings with the ensemble. Mr. Ormandy donated his yearly salary to a fund for student assistance. His own assistant conductor, William Smith, was assigned to rehearse the students weekly, and David Effron, who had joined the Curtis opera department in 1970, led them in intensive readings of the standard repertoire.

Concerts featuring the Curtis Orchestra were held at Curtis Hall with Messrs. Effron and Smith, opera coach Thomas Fulton or opera department head Max Rudolf on the podium. One memorable occasion was the February 4, 1973, concert at Philadelphia's Academy of Music, when Eugene Ormandy conducted the Curtis Symphony Orchestra in a program of Berlioz and Prokofiev, as well as Mozart's Piano Concerto in G major, K. 453, with Rudolf Serkin as soloist.

Messrs. Ormandy and Smith took particular interest in the many gifted Curtis musicians who won the Philadelphia Orchestra's annual student competition and, as a result, were given the opportunity to appear as soloists with the orchestra in its children's, junior and senior student concert series. For some, like violinist Nadja Salerno-Sonnenberg and pianist Marcantonio Barone, the opportunity came very young. And for a few, once was not enough. Michael Ludwig, who is today the Philadelphia Orchestra's associate concertmaster, became quite a familiar figure at Broad and Locust Streets, winning the competition at ages ten, fifteen and twenty.

Not surprisingly, the student competition has also been a stepping stone to the regular concert series. Mr. Smith first heard Korean violinist Young Uck Kim in 1963, when he was a contestant (and winner) in the junior division of the competition. So impressed was Mr. Smith with the Curtis student that he called "The Boss" at home; Mr. Ormandy immediately walked over to hear him. Five years later Mr. Kim made his professional debut with Eugene Ormandy and the Philadelphia Orchestra.

Perhaps Mr. Ormandy's greatest contribution to The Curtis Institute of Music was encouraging guest conductors of the Philadelphia Orchestra to work with the Curtis ensemble. Thus began a tradition that continues to this day. Claudio Abbado, István Kertész, Zubin Mehta, Riccardo Muti, Charles Dutoit and Rafael Frühbeck de Burgos were among the

An Artist of a Different Kind

No artist was better able to capture the uniqueness and eccentricities of the musicians of his time than American caricaturist Alfred Bendiner. In 1975 his widow presented The Curtis Institute of Music with twenty-seven drawings of famous individuals, created by her husband. The collection includes several Curtis-related personalities, from Leopold Stokowski to Rudolf Serkin, many of them signed by the subjects. The drawings were hung for the Golden Anniversary, remaining on permanent display.

conductors who gladly took on this assignment in the Ormandy years, many of them returning often.

The mutually satisfying relationship between the junior and the senior orchestra down the street had concrete results indeed: Fifty-four musicians on the roster of the Philadelphia Orchestra during the 1973/74 season were Curtis-trained, of whom ten were principals.

During the 1975/76 season, the Curtis Orchestra played for the first time at the Kennedy Center of the Performing Arts in Washington, D.C. Led by Alexander Schneider, the musicians presented an all-Haydn program, as part of a month-long festival of that composer's works.

Opera Returns to Center Stage

Rudolf Serkin restored opera to center stage at Curtis, inviting Max Rudolf to re-create and head a department devoted to operatic instruction and performance. The German-born conductor had been artistic administrator of the Metropolitan Opera under Rudolf Bing, where he conducted frequently; more recently he had been music director of the Cincinnati Symphony Orchestra. Mr. Rudolf was also charged with reviving the Curtis conducting department, which had been eliminated when Fritz Reiner left a generation before.

Max Rudolf assumed his position in 1970, asking Dino Yannopoulos, a longtime colleague at the Met, then residing in Munich, to become stage director. Serving as Mr. Rudolf's assistant was his protégé, David Effron; Mr. Effron came with experience as conductor and chorus master of the New York City Opera. Several of Max Rudolf's conducting students were chosen to act as coaches, and singers Margaret Harshaw and Charles Kullman of the Metropolitan Opera added their considerable experience to the team.

Students immersed themselves in every aspect of opera, from the learning of new roles to the mastery of foreign languages and body movement, including fencing. Some were accepted with very little stage experience, while others had appeared with smaller companies. Generally they were older than the usual Curtis population, with twenty-eight being the upper limit upon enrollment and only nine or ten accepted each year. During their Curtis training, students were introduced by Mr. Rudolf to a variety of professional contacts, including European agents from whom they might obtain engagements after graduation.

The results were remarkable, both in quality of performance and in the breadth and challenge of the works undertaken, among them: Wolf-Ferrari's *The School for Fathers*, Handel's *Rodelinda*, Richard Strauss' *Ariadne auf Naxos*, Britten's *The Rape of Lucretia* and Rossini's *Il Signor Bruschino*. Performances were held in a new opera rehearsal hall constructed in the

Alumnus Richard Goode conducts a master class at Curtis with student Anna Polonsky (1998).

mid-1960s above Curtis Hall, and outside the school in such venues as Drexel University and the Annenberg Center. Some operas were given in full, others excerpted, some presented with piano reductions with David Effron at the keyboard, others with the Curtis Orchestra. Critics and audiences alike proclaimed the Curtis operas to be among the most exciting offerings in the Philadelphia musical season.

At the close of the 1972/73 season, Max Rudolf left to take up another demanding assignment at the Met. Dino Yannopoulos then assumed directorship of the department, with Mr. Effron appointed conductor. Having worked closely with Mr. Rudolf, the new team maintained his philosophy, adding innovative productions to the Philadelphia season, many of which were given at the Walnut Street Theater.

Mr. Yannopoulos was particularly interested in rarely performed and contemporary works. He brought to Philadelphia the first performance in twenty years of Stravinsky's *The Rake's Progress*, a massive effort that spanned many months of planning and thirty-five-hour rehearsal weeks. Also produced under him were Cimarosa's *Il Matrimonio Segreto*, Rossini's *L'Italiana in Algeri* and Handel's *Xerxes*. Even in more popular works he tended to do the unusual, choosing a newly revised staging of Offenbach's *Les Contes d'Hoffmann* that had originated at an East Berlin company. Whether the opera was by Donizetti, Hindemith, Mozart or Massenet, it was bound to be thought out to the last detail, the last gesture.

Among the students who achieved successful operatic careers after this training were Katherine Ciesinski and Vinson Cole, who took the leading roles in a Curtis production of Massenet's *Werther*. Ms. Ciesinski, a 1974 Metropolitan Opera audition winner, was in her final year at Curtis when she was given only a week's notice to take over the leading role in Donizetti's *La Favorita*, which she had never sung, with the Opera Company of Philadelphia.

A Mecca for Chamber Music

As a masterful chamber musician, Rudolf Serkin was eager to make this form another area of focus during his Curtis directorship. His connection with the Marlboro School of Music and Festival in Vermont, as a founder as well as president and artistic director, was key to this goal.

Located in the foothills of the Green Mountains in Vermont on the campus of Marlboro College, the haven for chamber music had been created in 1951 by Mr. Serkin, his father-in-law Adolf Busch, the latter's brother, Hermann Busch, and their close friends, Marcel, Louis and Blanche Moyse. Its philosophy was complementary to that of Curtis, for here music was seen less as a profession than a passion, to be pursued not for a prescribed

Alumnus Peter Serkin, son of Rudolf Serkin, performs at the Marlboro School of Music and Festival.

period of study but for a lifetime. The setting was simple and rustic, with study and performance in a series of converted cow barns and farm buildings.

Quickly it became apparent that the students at Marlboro (who, like those at Curtis, seek entry rather than being recruited) were so gifted that a strict line of demarcation between them and the faculty was unnecessary. Rather, all were considered to be "participants," the younger musicians working closely with their more experienced colleagues to plumb the treasures of the vast chamber music literature. In this bucolic and idealistic setting, Rudolf Serkin was at his happiest — and most informal, helping to clear away the chairs after concerts and taking it stoically when younger participants showed their affection by pelting him with napkin balls in the dining room.

It was Mr. Serkin's hope, as Curtis director, that students would study at Marlboro for as many years as they attended Curtis — and a large number have continued to do so. Each summer, in fact, perhaps one-quarter of the Marlboro community is composed of Curtis students and graduates.

As chamber music became an ever more important focus at Curtis, key new faculty members were engaged. The four members of the Guarneri String Quartet were among the first to be invited by Mr. Serkin, in 1968. Two years later, Mischa Schneider, the Russian-born graduate of the Leipzig Conservatory who had been cellist with the esteemed Budapest String

Quartet for over three decades, joined the faculty. Violinist Yumi Ninomiya Scott of the Curtis String Quartet arrived the same year.

Felix Galimir, the violinist who, with his three sisters, had made up the Galimir Quartet, joined the faculty in 1972. Three decades of students have been privileged to study chamber music under this Viennese musician who worked closely with some of the greatest musicians of the twentieth century — Webern, Berg, Milhaud, Ravel and Toscanini among them.

Also new to the faculty was Jaime Laredo, a 1959 Curtis graduate, whose brilliant career as a soloist and conductor has been matched by his commitment to chamber music. Mr. Laredo heads the annual New York String Seminar at Carnegie Hall and tours the world in a trio with pianist Joseph Kalichstein and cellist Sharon Robinson as well as in solo and conducting capacities. He also plays frequently in various combinations with pianist Emanuel Ax, violinist Isaac Stern and cellist Yo-Yo Ma. A double concerto for Mr. Laredo and Ms. Robinson by Ned Rorem was premiered in 1998.

John Weaver, another 1959 graduate and student of organist Alexander McCurdy, also began to teach at Curtis during the Serkin leadership. A recitalist, choir director, composer and recording artist, Mr. Weaver is also chair of the organ department of Juilliard. Another addition to the faculty was Edward Aldwell, co-author of the textbook *Harmony and Voice Leading*, as well as a renowned interpreter of the works of J. S. Bach.

T-Shirts and Ponytails

A new atmosphere of openness and informality characterized the Serkin directorship. Whereas in the past The Institute had kept to itself (indeed, one music critic likened it to "a great limestone turtle" that withdrew into itself), now the doors were opened to music lovers throughout the city of Philadelphia. This came as a pleasant surprise to many Philadelphians, who previously had not realized what a cultural treasure was located on Rittenhouse Square.

The new audiences were treated to more eclectic programs than those of the past, with repertoire and instruments mixed. Posterity was also served, for, starting with the 1968/69 academic year, the recording of performances in Curtis Hall, curtailed since the war years, was resumed; a few years later the opera department began to videotape its own productions. The library moved to Knapp Hall, which had been repurchased from the Elizabeth Arden Company in 1969; it was outfitted with equipment for viewing, and the listening facilities were expanded in 1974.

Particularly visible was the change in attire at the school, which took on a decidedly more casual tone — except when Mrs. Zimbalist was in town. T-shirts spelling out the school's

Mr. Sehrkind in Opera

Director Rudolf Serkin on one occasion found himself cast in an opera. In a 1974 Curtis presentation of Mozart's singspiel, "The Impresario," the students changed the role of impresario to that of music school director, naming him Mr. Sehrkind. The fictional director's lot in life was to suffer the tantrums of two rival sopranos.

Violinist Felix Galimir has brought his remarkable knowledge of chamber music literature to Curtis students.

Pianist Mieczyslaw Horszowski with violinist Jaime Laredo.

name in gold were designed, and the school's dean, Peter Schoenbach (son of bassoon faculty member Sol Schoenbach) arranged to have one on Director Serkin's desk, awaiting his return from a tour. Beards and long hair were the norm; indeed, the director's own son, Peter, by then a well-established artist, would often appear on stage sporting a pony tail, baggy pants and an Indian shirt — quite a contrast to the conservative Middle European appearance of Mr. Serkin, Sr.

Also of increasing concern at Curtis was the students' emotional well-being. A student lounge was created in the basement when the library moved in 1974. Practical help was offered, especially to foreign students, on everything from legal matters to finances, social life to health, and tutors were on call for those whose English-speaking ability was limited. Recognizing that emotional stress was apt to result when students were transplanted into a new culture, the administration engaged a psychologist.

Special arrangements were also made for students who wished to study certain academic subjects at outside institutions, such as the University of Pennsylvania and Swarthmore College.

As Philadelphians began to know Curtis, so did Curtis become more a part of Philadelphia. A student concert bureau, which had not existed since the late 1930s, when Thomas D. Perry, Jr. (later, executive director of the Boston Symphony) drove the students to and from their performances in a Ford sedan garaged across Locust Street, was re-established. The students were once again enabled to perform in various settings — albeit minus the Ford transportation — including senior citizen organizations, drug rehabilitation centers, community functions and with community orchestras. Thus they gained broader experience of the realities outside their small and privileged world, while helping to create new audiences for classical music.

The groundwork was laid in the Serkin years for what eventually became a formalized program of fundraising. It was now apparent that, while the school had no debts, its future as a scholarship-only institution was far from secure, for the school's expanded programs — notably in the opera department — were very expensive.

A Golden Anniversary

The fiftieth anniversary of The Curtis Institute of Music, in the 1974/75 season, provided an ideal occasion for a celebration of the school's origins and its continued excellence in the face of Depression, World War II, lessening financial resources and a world in which the arts were being increasingly and alarmingly undervalued.

The celebration, which took place throughout the academic year, was organized by a key member of the Curtis administration, manager and artistic coordinator Anthony P.

Checchia, a Curtis bassoon alumnus who later founded the highly successful Philadelphia Chamber Music Society and also serves as administrator at Marlboro. It began with a series of recitals at the school, given by distinguished alumni. A fall orchestra concert was led by William Steinberg. The opera department presented three fully-staged productions in English at the Walnut Street Theater, as well as a number of offerings in The Institute's own studio, including Wagner's *Die Walküre*. Throughout the year, works by leading composer graduates of Curtis, among them Vincent Persichetti, George Walker, Gian Carlo Menotti, Samuel Barber, George Rochberg, Ned Rorem, Leonard Bernstein and Lukas Foss, were performed.

By this time, master classes were often held at Curtis, but for the anniversary year a highly intensive series was developed under the direction of three eminent European musicians. The artist-teachers invited to supervise the series were Viennese pianist Paul Badura-Skoda, Russian violinist Leonid Kogan and French flutist Marcel Moyse. Each came for two to three weeks, and several of the events were open to other area music schools and universities.

Arriving at Curtis in March 1975 for his own master class was the Russian cello virtuoso Mstislav Rostropovich, who thoroughly charmed the community of students and faculty with his all-enveloping warmth and his idiomatic — albeit sometimes incomprehensible — English. Politics were not discussed, but many people thought of this gentle man's courage in opposing the repression of artists in his Russian homeland.

The same year also marked the seventy-fifth anniversary of Mieczyslaw Horszowski's debut in Vienna. To celebrate this, the master pianist, now eighty-three, appeared three times: in recital, in concert with the Curtis Orchestra, playing the first performance of an unpublished Mendelssohn piano concerto, and in a Music from Marlboro chamber concert.

Another project of the fiftieth anniversary season was the mechanical restoration and enlarging of the organ in Curtis Hall. The project was supervised by the former tonal director of the Aeolian-Skinner Company, the firm that had built the instrument. In November 1975, John Weaver presented a recital that clearly revealed the success of the project. Indeed, it was agreed that the initial beauty and performance capabilities of the organ had not only been equaled but exceeded.

The celebration reached its peak with a gala fiftieth anniversary weekend, from February 28 through March 2, 1975, during which time a dinner, attended by 750, was held in the Bellevue-Stratford Hotel ballroom, and a concert was performed at the Academy of Music. Ruth Seltzer, the *Philadelphia Inquirer*'s society doyenne, wrote of the dinner: "So many luminaries are expected that the seating committee is in a dither." And no wonder. Where to place the likes of Maestro and Mrs. Ormandy, Riccardo Muti, Governor and Mrs. Milton J.

The Guarneri String Quartet, formed at Marlboro in 1964, with violinists Arnold Steinhardt and John Dalley, cellist David Soyer and violist Michael Tree. All four have served as Curtis faculty members (1988).

Shapp, and Nancy Hanks, chairman of the National Endowment for the Arts? Or the 300 illustrious alumni who had come from around the world to attend the first Curtis reunion ever? This large turnout was thanks to alumnus/faculty member John de Lancie, principal oboist of the Philadelphia Orchestra, who developed and headed the first alumni association in the school's history.

Boris Goldovsky served, with typical wit, as master of ceremonies at the dinner, and waves of applause greeted faculty members from the early years, such as Renée Longy and Emanuel Zetlin. This was the occasion on which guest speaker Leonard Bernstein spoke so candidly about his own years as a Curtis student. Mr. Menotti produced yet another staging of his delightful musical setting of the decidedly unmusical Curtis catalogue, performed by three male singers, bassoon and piano. (The three singers might never have been accepted at Curtis as students — let alone faculty members — for their vocal ability, but in this setting Orlando Cole, Alexander McCurdy and Boris Goldovsky were cheered loudly.) And, as if there hadn't been enough fun, Jacques Offenbach's comic opera *R.S.V.P., or An Evening at Mr. Cauliflower's*, was presented in an English translation by Dino Yannopoulos, with graduates Gianna Rolandi and Vinson Cole in the leads.

The March 2 concert held at the Academy of Music was dedicated to the memory of the founder of The Curtis Institute of Music and its president for forty-five years, Mary Louise Curtis Bok Zimbalist. The all-Beethoven program included the Seventh Symphony, the Third *Leonore* Overture and the Fifth Piano Concerto, *(Emperor)*, with soloist Rudolf Serkin. Eugene Ormandy conducted the Curtis Symphony Orchestra.

Philadelphia's Academy of Music was sold out for that festive evening, and the house was replete with musical luminaries. Indeed, it was impossible to determine whether there was more talent on one side of the footlights than the other. Comments were heard that if a natural — or unnatural — disaster were to destroy the Academy that night, music history would be set back a hundred years.

Rudolf Serkin resigned as Curtis director in May 1975, having previously stated that he would see The Institute through its fiftieth year. During the interim period when a new director was actively sought, the president of the Curtis board, M. Todd Cooke, assumed a leadership role.

Mr. Serkin and his family moved their headquarters from Rittenhouse Square to their farm in Brattleboro, Vermont, which remained the center of his personal and professional life. His association with the Marlboro School of Music would continue until his death in 1991. This was the place that embodied Rudolf Serkin's deepest beliefs about music, and here he would continue to be greeted with love and gratitude by the ever-growing Curtis Institute family.

Jenny at Curtis

There she was, carrot-topped, wrapped in furs, and wreathed in cigarette smoke. The indomitable entertainer Lotte Lenya, widow of composer Kurt Weill, came to Curtis in 1976 to observe rehearsals for a performance of her late husband's music, to be given as a benefit for the school. The famous "Jenny" of "The Threepenny Opera," whose name is inextricably linked onstage with that of her husband, was guest of honor at the performance, delighting guests when she sang a chorus of "Mack the Knife."

Director John de Lancie, on left, and composer Gian Carlo Menotti (1978).

Chapter Six

The de Lancie Years

A NEW MANDATE

In February 1977, the seventh director of The Curtis Institute of Music took office. California native John de Lancie was the first graduate in the school's history to be chosen as its leader.

He had come to Curtis at age fifteen, a student of the great French oboist Marcel Tabuteau, principal player of the Philadelphia Orchestra. Upon graduating in 1940, Mr. de Lancie became a member of the Pittsburgh Symphony under Fritz Reiner and, in summer, of the Robin Hood Dell Orchestra in Philadelphia. In 1942 he joined the U.S. Army, where he was a member of the Army Band, serving in the European Theater. At the end of the war Eugene Ormandy appointed Mr. de Lancie associate solo oboist of the Philadelphia Orchestra. When Marcel Tabuteau retired in 1954, Mr. de Lancie became principal player, as well as instructor of oboe on the Curtis faculty.

John de Lancie is one of the foremost oboists of our time. In a recently published tribute, Richard Woodhams, his student and successor both at Curtis and at the Philadelphia Orchestra, described Mr. de Lancie's playing as being characterized by "the direct, sincere delivery of sensitive musical ideas," his breath control so complete as to humble the most confident of students. Mr. de Lancie recorded several concertos for oboe and orchestra with the Philadelphia Orchestra and with the London Symphony Orchestra, and he enhanced the literature of his chosen instrument through commissions. One major work, written for him at his suggestion in 1945/46, was a concerto for oboe by Richard Strauss. Mr. de Lancie was a founding member of the Philadelphia Woodwind Quintet, composed of musicians in the Philadelphia Orchestra. On the retirement of flutist William Kincaid in 1967, he took over the woodwind classes at Curtis.

When he became director of Curtis, John de Lancie was involved with the school in many ways beyond teaching. He had been elected to the board of trustees and entrusted

Vladimir Sokoloff, whose record as Curtis accompanist is unmatched in number of performances, plays here for alumna soprano Anna Moffo (1985).

Alumnus Leonard Bernstein rehearses the Curtis Orchestra for its sixtieth anniversary concert in 1984.

with the formation of a new alumni association, of which he became president. The task of locating alumni from around the world and linking them anew with their alma mater was a massive one, and Mr. de Lancie carried it out with great success. A strong alumni presence during the school's fiftieth year celebration was the first notable result.

As a teacher, John de Lancie has been described as an unrelenting taskmaster, a perfectionist who minced no words. Oboist Woodhams recalls that Mr. de Lancie required traditional French solfège of his Curtis students for three years, "ending in exercises in ungodly keys with long-abandoned clefs." Despite these rigors, Mr. de Lancie was greatly respected by his young oboists because he demanded of them no more than he did of himself. And, after they'd gotten through the relentless repetition of note after note, phrase after phrase, they were treated to the friendly, fatherly qualities of the slim, patrician man whose devotion to them — and to The Curtis Institute of Music — was unquestioned.

The school that Mr. de Lancie inherited from Rudolf Serkin was one of artistic excellence. Its orchestra had gained from a strengthened relationship with the Philadelphia Orchestra. The productions of the opera department at the Walnut Street Theater were elaborate and on a very high professional level. But opera was a deficit operation, costing more money than the board felt was warranted. The need was also perceived for a greater sense of structure within the school and for a more even-handed balance between departments.

John de Lancie's mandate was to restore the school's financial stability without threatening its major tenets, in particular the policy of merit-based full-tuition scholarships for all students. In order to devote his full attention to this task, Mr. de Lancie retired from his position with the Philadelphia Orchestra in the same year he became Curtis director.

To Our Valentine

Sergiu Celibidache remained something of an enigma to Curtis students even after three weeks of intensive study, but their ways were probably just as strange to him. On Valentine's Day the students presented the Romanian maestro with a large card featuring the cartoon "Peanuts," that read: "There are some things which just can't be put into words."

Early in the de Lancie administration, the famous Burrell collection of Wagner materials that had been purchased by Mrs. Bok was put up for auction at Christie's in New York. Its sale in 1978 grossed close to $1.4 million for the Curtis endowment.

In 1979, two years after Leopold Stokowski's death at age ninety-five, The Institute received the conductor's library of 1,500 orchestral scores, his transcriptions and a collection of percussion instruments (including gongs and chimes from Bali and Tibet). These were to be housed at Curtis and made available to orchestras and scholars. A dedication ceremony was held on February 26, 1980, with Edwin Heilakka named as curator.

New Directions and Old Loyalties

Academic studies were pursued in a more formal manner during the de Lancie administration, with the arrival of Joan Hutton Landis, a critic, essayist, poet and actress, who holds a Ph.D. from Bryn Mawr College in English literature. Efforts were initiated by the director and the school's executive assistant (now dean), Robert Fitzpatrick, a 1968 clarinet alumnus, that would eventually lead to accreditation of Curtis by the National Association of Schools of Music.

Mr. de Lancie wanted to offer maximum opportunity for students in live performance. An average of sixty recitals was given at the school each academic year, and there was a monthly chamber music series at the Federal Reserve Bank Building, free of charge and open to the public, as well as another series for the medical staff at Hahnemann Hospital. New York's Carnegie Recital Hall was the venue for yet another series of student concerts. At the same time, stricter controls were imposed on performances outside the school's purview through a written process requiring permission of the faculty.

Another of Mr. de Lancie's goals was to return Curtis to the air, in a fashion similar to the series of broadcasts heard in the 1930s. Negotiations were held with Philadelphia's public radio station, WUHY, resulting in a weekly stereo broadcast, "Concerts at Curtis," beginning with the 1977/78 season, which included student recitals as well as orchestral, vocal and chamber music performances, some involving guest conductors. The fact of these being live, without the chance for retakes and tape editing, imposed the kind of discipline the students would need as professionals.

In the area of vocal studies, Mr. de Lancie felt that he could best address the school's primary purpose, as well as its financial concerns, by concentrating on preparation instead of performance. Voice students were now younger, less experienced, but with fine potential for future careers. New to the faculty was baritone Todd Duncan, the opera

Jorge Bolet, then head of the Curtis piano faculty, after a performance in Curtis Hall (1978).

Faculty member William Smith rehearses with alumnus/faculty member Aaron Rosand (1984).

1939 Curtis alumnus Shura Cherkassky, on left, reunites with pianist/composer Abram Chasins, a fellow alumnus who was on the Curtis faculty in its early years (1984).

singer/concert artist who had become famous for creating the title role of Porgy in George Gershwin's opera *Porgy and Bess*. Sylvan Levin, formerly a close associate of Leopold Stokowski at Curtis, returned as repertory coach.

Taking over the opera department was another familiar face: Boris Goldovsky, a 1934 Curtis graduate. While a conducting student of Fritz Reiner, Mr. Goldovsky had been assigned operatic coaching at the school. Subsequently he became director of opera at the Cleveland Institute of Music and at the New England Conservatory, and he founded and directed the New England Opera. To countless fans around the country, his was the radio voice heard during Saturday afternoon Metropolitan Opera broadcasts — a sophisticated, erudite exponent of his art and an unparalleled raconteur.

Under Mr. Goldovsky, the opera department now presented public performances in English in the school's own theater, Studio II-J, as well as at the Plays and Players Theater and the auditorium of the John Wanamaker department store. Sometimes the Curtis Orchestra was in the pit, and at other times stage director Goldovsky was a one-man orchestra, seated at the piano. Scenes from a variety of operas alternated with full productions. Among the works given in full were Puccini's *Madama Butterfly*, Humperdinck's *Hansel and Gretel*, Debussy's *L'Enfant Prodigue*, Rossini's *A Turk in Italy*, Floyd's *Susannah*, Britten's *Albert Herring* and Rimsky-Korsakov's *Mozart and Salieri*. Gian Carlo Menotti was brought in for a production of *Amelia Goes to the Ball*.

In his desire to enhance the sense of pride and tradition at Curtis, Mr. de Lancie carried out several projects. He had the main floor's former library made into an elegant drawing room that featured an ornate piano from the Curtis mansion, naming this the Bok Room. He also developed a commemorative series of concerts, honoring distinguished faculty members of the past (some still very much alive), at the same time dedicating studios in their name.

The subject of the first commemorative day, held October 28, 1977, was harpist Carlos Salzedo, who had died in 1961. Alumni came with their harps from near and far to reminisce and to dedicate a studio to "Cher maître," as he was known. The sounds emanating from Curtis on that day must have echoed through Rittenhouse Square like an angelic choir. It all ended with a seven-harp ensemble conducted by the Philadelphia Orchestra's first harpist Marilyn Costello, in a performance of Salzedo's own work, *Bolmimerie*.

Similarly, the school honored its former director Efrem Zimbalist, oboist Marcel Tabuteau, pianist Mieczyslaw Horszowski and composer Samuel Barber, whose tribute was timed to his seventieth birthday (and who died the next year). One can only imagine how moved Mr. Barber must have been to hear fellow classmates from the class of 1934 in performance of his own works — Rose Bampton singing *Dover Beach*, and Orlando Cole playing his cello sonata with Vladimir Sokoloff at the piano.

Lesson with a Master

Richard Woodhams, writing about his Curtis oboe teacher, John de Lancie, in the publication "The Double Reed," described a lesson as follows:

"One morning at Mr. de Lancie's home I played the Barret Grand Study #12, 'Lento Vigoroso.' In the middle section, replete with trills, I played mordents instead, thinking it too fast to be played with real trills. He stopped me, asked me for my oboe, and, sitting in his easy chair and obviously having recently emerged from a deep and much-needed slumber, proceeded to play the passage faster than I did with perfectly even and well-delineated trills. He handed me back my oboe with an expression of quizzical, mild disdain."

Alumnus pianist Peter Serkin, on left, chats with Curtis director John de Lancie (1984).

Faculty member Max Rudolf with conducting student Michael Stern (1985).

Gian Carlo Menotti's oeuvre was recognized, also on his seventieth birthday, with three concerts; one of them featured that much-loved Curtis tradition, Mr. Menotti's own setting of the Curtis catalogue, with the venerable chamber musician Felix Galimir in an uncharacteristic singing role. Though not formally part of the commemorative series, a tribute concert to flutist William Kincaid was presented at the Port of History Museum, with two eminent flutists in performance: Curtis faculty member Julius Baker and the French master Jean-Pierre Rampal.

The Curtis Institute of Music honored the remarkable pianist Mieczyslaw Horszowski in April 1981, when he was eighty-nine years of age, with a concert of four-hand piano music by alumni. That evening the shy and unassuming guest of honor was soloist in a Mozart concerto, with the Curtis Orchestra under the direction of William Smith.

Alumna Susan Starr is greeted by alumnus Leonard Bernstein at The Institute's sixtieth year celebration in 1984.

Orchestral Triumphs

Mr. Smith, a modest man of encyclopedic musical knowledge with a reputation for being able to conduct virtually any piece of music at a moment's notice, continued to provide rigorous training to the Curtis Orchestra. Under him, the ensemble undertook such ambitious efforts as a series of back-to-back concerts honoring the centennial of Igor Stravinsky's birth in 1982.

Of particular note was an invitation for the student orchestra to perform in the 1980 Annual American Composers Competition at the John F. Kennedy Center for the Performing Arts in Washington, D.C. The works to be played, each one a contender for the annual Friedheim Award, were difficult, representing the broad spectrum of contemporary schools of composition. A crisis was narrowly averted at the 1980 concert when its scheduled conductor, Lukas Foss, fell ill. Robert Fitzpatrick, who had been principal conductor of the Orchestra Society of Philadelphia and was now on The Institute's administrative staff, stepped in at the last minute. The concert was broadcast live by National Public Radio and was heard abroad through the Voice of America. (Mr. Fitzpatrick conducted the Curtis Orchestra at the same competition in 1984 and 1988.)

Guest conductors engaged by the Philadelphia Orchestra somehow managed to find the time for rehearsals and performances at Curtis (concerts took place, variously, in Curtis Hall, the Academy of Music and the Port of History Museum). Among them was the Philadelphia Orchestra's music-director-to-be Riccardo Muti, in interpretations hailed as vibrant and elegant, of Mozart, Beethoven, Mendelssohn and Mussorgsky. Rafael Frühbeck de Burgos led an electrifying performance of Stravinsky's *The Rite of Spring*, and the nonagenarian French conductor Paul Paray captivated students and audience in two appearances.

Violinist Jaime Laredo, on left, and pianist Vladimir Sokoloff, both longtime members of the Curtis family, share a hug.

Romanian conductor Sergiu Celibidache came to Curtis for a three-week residency in 1984, which culminated in two now-historic concerts.

Alumnus/faculty member Jascha Brodsky gives a lesson to Martin Chalifour, a 1984 Curtis alumnus (1984).

No concert brought back more memories of the early years than the centennial tribute concert to Leopold Stokowski, held April 18, 1982, at the Academy of Music, with Zubin Mehta, then head of the New York Philharmonic, conducting. All the works performed were associated with "Stoki" — Bach and Wagner in his own orchestrations and excerpts from the opera he brought to America: Berg's *Wozzeck*. The performance was broadcast live and transmitted nationwide over National Public Radio stations.

One more concert took place during the de Lancie administration that will long be remembered in the annals of American music. In February 1984, the school's sixtieth year, the reclusive, seventy-one-year-old Romanian conductor Sergiu Celibidache arrived to prepare the students for two concerts, one at the Port of History Museum in Philadelphia and a subsequent repeat at Carnegie Hall in New York.

At the time, the conductor was leader of the Munich Philharmonic, but his enduring fame derived from his directorship of the Berlin Philharmonic. Having disowned his own recordings and refusing to do new ones, Mr. Celibidache was virtually unknown to American audiences.

Negotiations began a good year-and-a-half before the conductor's arrival. Mr. de Lancie was eager to engage him, not only for his great musical gifts but because he always insisted on a great number of rehearsals (more than any professional orchestra would accept) and thus was prepared to settle in at Curtis, rather than to drop by for a long weekend. Interestingly, what seemed to have convinced Mr. Celibidache to accept the invitation was a performance of the Curtis String Quartet in Europe.

And so he arrived, a big-framed, swarthy, white-haired master with eagle eyes, who bore a striking resemblance to the elderly Franz Liszt. The three weeks of his tenure were among the most arduous in The Institute's history. In all, there were seventeen rehearsals, along with many lectures — some lasting three hours — which combined spiritual mysticism and phenomenology, a branch of philosophy close to the conductor's heart.

Sarcastic, capable of stinging rebukes and harsh judgments (the last movement of Beethoven's Fifth Symphony was "terrible music" and Arturo Toscanini was "not a musician"), Mr. Celibidache alienated some members of the Curtis student body, as well as other music students and musicians who had come from afar to audit his classes and rehearsals. But in the end, the conductor's extraordinary technique, his remarkable sense of color, of intonation, balance and phrasing, turned most of them into believers. Even if they did not always agree with his message, they acknowledged his deep devotion to music.

Critics at the two concerts could hardly find the words to express their excitement. "The result was about as revelatory an experience, both thrilling and thought-provoking, as this writer has encountered in twenty-five years of regular concert-going," wrote John Rockwell in the *New York Times* of the February 24 concert in Carnegie Hall.

Mr. Celibidache was delighted. "These American students, they are wonderful," he said.

At Home and Across the Atlantic

There were a number of new and renewed faculty appointments in the de Lancie years. Upon the departure of Rudolf Serkin, the Cuban pianist Jorge Bolet returned to head the piano department. One of the major keyboard artists of his time, Mr. Bolet was especially regarded for his playing of Liszt, to which he brought technical mastery and romantic panache.

In 1981, Mr. de Lancie invited Gary Graffman, whose concert career had been curtailed by an injury to his right hand, to join the piano faculty. Although he would not be taking on students of his own at the time, Mr. Graffman would listen to other teachers' students. The thinking behind this admittedly unusual assignment was that nonagenarian Horszowski would not, alas, teach forever, and Mr. de Lancie wanted someone of the highest caliber to be in readiness to replace him.

Several first-desk players at the Philadelphia Orchestra joined the faculty, including a onetime Zimbalist student, concertmaster Norman Carol, who took on the teaching of orchestral repertoire to strings. Curtis alumnus Julius Baker, who had been solo flutist of the Pittsburgh Symphony and the Chicago Symphony and now held that position at the New York Philharmonic, arrived in 1980.

In April 1981, the renowned violinist and longtime Curtis faculty member Ivan Galamian died. Szymon Goldberg, former concertmaster of the Berlin Philharmonic, and Aaron Rosand, a Curtis alumnus who had studied with Efrem Zimbalist, were appointed to the violin faculty. When Mr. Rosand appeared in recital in Curtis Hall on April 19, 1982, after an absence from that stage of more than three decades, his audience gave him a triumphant homecoming. Mr. Rosand played encore after encore, stating that he was prepared to stay until morning. It was reported by a witness that, on hearing this offer, the soloist's faithful accompanist, Vladimir Sokoloff, was filled with "righteous terror, for he hastily closed the piano and fled from the stage."

In the area of composition, Ned Rorem joined the faculty in 1980. The Indiana-born musician had won the Pulitzer Prize in music just three years before. His large oeuvre comprises symphonies, piano concerti, operas, ballets, choral works, songs and song cycles, and he is among the most frequently performed of contemporary composers in the United States.

John de Lancie's commitment to Curtis students extended to summers, during which he initiated a program of European travel and performance for chamber groups such as the Kasimir Quartet, composed of young women in their senior year at Curtis. Mr. and Mrs. de Lancie accompanied the ensemble to Europe in 1979, where it performed eighteen times to critical acclaim.

These appearances increased The Institute's visibility abroad and helped the school win a prestigious invitation from the Evian International Music Festival, located in a resort

A Nose Across the Page

Leopold Stokowski's library, acquired by Curtis after his death, had much emotional importance to the school, especially to the school's orchestra librarian Nancy Shear, who had known "Stoki" since she was a teenager. She had worked for him as a music secretary at the Philadelphia Orchestra and later in New York. Their last meeting occurred one month before his death, at which time he was planning to resume recording. Ms. Shear recalled that some of the scores looked like children's scrapbooks because the conductor had taken to pasting mementos, like photographs of the composers, on the pages. Among her jobs was erasing the notations that players had added, which were not always flattering to their leader. One of the players must have been an artist at heart, for he (or she) had drawn a caricature of Stokowski in a Beethoven score, with the nose going all the way across some eighteen pages.

Curtis cello alumnus Lynn Harrell, on left, greets his onetime teacher, alumnus Orlando Cole (1984).

Faculty member Max Rudolf rehearses the Curtis Orchestra (1985).

Alumnus Gian Carlo Menotti with alumnus/faculty member Norman Carol, then concertmaster of the Philadelphia Orchestra (1981).

town on the French bank of Lake Léman, near Geneva, to play during the annual event in May 1983. An invitation was issued again in 1984 — the beginning of a long and fine association. In that second year the Orchestra was seen throughout France via the popular monthly television program, *Le Grand Echiquier*.

The philosophy guiding the Evian Festival was to combine the talents of outstanding young musicians with prominent soloists and conductors. The first year of Curtis' participation was the eighth year of the Festival, and the students performed four programs, one of them with Dean Fitzpatrick conducting and Oscar Shumsky playing the Beethoven Violin Concerto.

The trip, according to an account by Edwin Heilakka, then orchestra librarian, began with high drama when Paul Roby, a violin student, lost control of his bicycle going down an S-shaped mountain road into town, hit a stone wall and lost consciousness. The determined violinist, who was rescued by fellow student Michael Stern, was at rehearsal the next morning. A second near-disaster was the confiscation of all the music plus 6,600 pounds of equipment by customs officials, who claimed that an official document was missing. Once again a crisis was averted, with the truck arriving just in time for rehearsal. Even the weather conspired to create havoc, with almost constant rain for three weeks, causing as many colds as there were musicians.

None of these soap-opera complications dampened spirits. The students didn't even quit at curtain time, for, having decided that the cocktail pianist in one of the local hotels was simply unacceptable, they obtained permission from management to take over after he'd retired at 11 p.m. It was quite a festival.

In 1984, the sixtieth year of The Curtis Institute of Music, many special events were held, including a week of concerts in April at The Institute and in the Grand Court of the John Wanamaker store, featuring numerous alumni. Listeners heard pianists Shura Cherkassky, Peter Serkin and Lee Luvisi and soprano Gianna Rolandi. The Muir String Quartet, whose members had met at Curtis in the 1970s and which had since won the Naumburg Chamber Music Award, performed. Violinist Henri Temianka, who had been a Curtis student in the school's first year, played, as did violinist Rafael Druian and cellist Lynn Harrell. The week ended with an orchestral concert at the Academy of Music, the podium being shared by Leonard Bernstein and William Smith, and two soloists, Aaron Rosand and Susan Starr.

As Rudolf Serkin had seen The Curtis Institute of Music through its half-century mark, so John de Lancie did for the sixtieth year. Mr. de Lancie left his position as Curtis director following the school's graduating ceremonies in May 1985. It was announced by the board chairman, A. Margaret Bok, daughter-in-law of the late Mrs. Zimbalist and widow of Mrs. Zimbalist's son Cary, that interim management would be provided by faculty members Vladimir Sokoloff and Orlando Cole and a few members of the administrative staff.

Young at Heart

At eighty-six, an age when most have long since retired from the concert stage, Mieczyslaw Horszowski made his debut with the Philadelphia Orchestra as soloist in Mozart's Piano Concerto in B-flat, K. 595. This was his first collaboration with conductor Eugene Ormandy, who observed his own seventy-ninth birthday at one of the performances, making him a junior partner to his soloist. Mr. Horszowski defied statistics once again, in his eighties, by marrying for the first time. His bride was Italian-born Bice Costa, also a pianist. When the legendary musician's sight became poor, preventing him from reading music, she would refresh his memory by going to the piano and playing the passages he requested.

Director/alumnus/pianist Gary Graffman, violinist Isaac Stern and cellist Mstislav Rostropovich in the Bok Room (1990).

Chapter Seven

The Graffman Years

T

A HALF-CENTURY ODYSSEY

The seven-year-old piano student who waited his turn to audition in the vast paneled drawing room of The Curtis Institute of Music back in 1935 was a self-described "dragon slayer." Neither the fact that he hadn't had time to warm up, nor the presence of the renowned Josef Hofmann (whom the boy addressed in fluent Russian), intimidated Gary Graffman, about to become a student of the revered and feared Isabelle Vengerova.

It was an auspicious beginning to a career that would take the pianist around the world and back home to the very same conservatory from which he had graduated in 1946. In June 1986, fifty years after having been accepted as a Curtis student, Gary Graffman was chosen to head the school, with the title of artistic director.

In the meantime he had enjoyed great professional success. After graduating from Curtis and making his debut with the Philadelphia Orchestra, the young musician continued his studies with Vladimir Horowitz and at Marlboro with Rudolf Serkin. The Leventritt Award launched him onto the international circuit, and for the next three decades he toured almost constantly. His recorded legacy with the "Big Five" orchestras stands as testimony to a man who, in the words of a *Washington Post* critic, is "one of the towering musicians of our time."

Through all this, Gary Graffman remained close to his alma mater. One of his fond memories is of the school's fiftieth anniversary celebration, during which then-director Serkin invited him to play a recital. On learning that the date chosen for this appearance was just a few days after the pianist's New York recital, Mr. Serkin beamed. "That's wonderful!" he said. "Your Carnegie Hall recital will be a perfect tryout for Curtis!" And, reports Mr. Graffman, although the Carnegie Hall experience helped, he was still nervous at the thought of playing for the Curtis family.

In 1979 something happened that, with a lesser artist, might have signaled an end to a major career but, in Gary Graffman's case, meant the beginning of a new and rich one.

It was then that his performing activities were rudely interrupted by an ailment afflicting the fourth and fifth fingers of his right hand; this may have resulted from the spraining of a knuckle some fifteen years earlier. In any event, Mr. Graffman was no longer able to play the two-handed literature.

Instead, he began to perform with the left hand alone, a career that has brought him acclaim with a different repertoire and recording legacy. Not only did he master concertos for the left hand by such composers as Ravel, Prokofiev, Britten, Korngold and Richard Strauss, but he championed new works as well. In 1993 Mr. Graffman's performing and academic careers converged in a particularly felicitous manner when he joined conductor André Previn and the Curtis Orchestra for the world premiere in Philadelphia of the Piano Concerto No. 4 (for left hand) by Curtis faculty member and Pulitzer Prize winner, Ned Rorem. The work was dedicated to Mr. Graffman, whose subsequent performance at Carnegie Hall was described by *The New York Times* as "electrifying."

Invited to join the Curtis faculty during Mr. de Lancie's directorship, Mr. Graffman continues to teach a small number of piano students. His office/studio is an oasis of tranquillity — wood-paneled walls and Oriental rugs, windows framed with gold damask drapes, a marble fireplace. The piano, donated by an alumnus, is a beautifully carved Steinway grand.

In 1989, the title of director was reinstated for Mr. Graffman, and six years later he was also named president, the first time in Curtis history that the school's leader was thus honored. In 1991, the State of Pennsylvania presented President/Director Graffman with its Governor's Award, in recognition of his many contributions to the arts.

Gary Graffman's non-musical interests include ancient Chinese art, notably ceramics from the Han to the early Ming dynasties, which he studied at Columbia University, learning a bit of the Mandarin language as well. While nobody is surprised to hear him teach Russian-speaking students in their (and his) mother tongue, comments made by him in Mandarin to Chinese students often elicit startled giggles.

The Curtis leader wears all this erudition lightly. Though his standards of musicianship are rigorous and uncompromising, he is approachable and warm, with an endless store of anecdotes and a sharp wit, directed as often to himself as to others. These qualities are apparent in Mr. Graffman's amusing memoir, *I Really Should Be Practicing*, published by Doubleday in 1981. Mr. Graffman maintains an "open-door" policy, scheduling weekly periods when students may freely visit him to share concerns and make suggestions.

Crucial to the success of The Institute in the last decade-and-a-half has been the farsightedness displayed by the administration and by the Board of Trustees, which currently is headed by Dr. Milton L. Rock, a Philadelphia businessman well known for his commitment to the arts. The development of a long-range plan was undertaken with the mission of assuring

Yuri Temirkanov, a frequent guest conductor at The Institute, works with the Curtis Symphony Orchestra (1992).

A Lifetime Opportunity

In April 1993 a twenty-one-year-old Curtis pianist, Meng-Chieh Liu, from Taiwan, was given a remarkable opportunity. Three hours before a scheduled solo appearance on the All-Star Forum series at Philadelphia's Academy of Music, pianist André Watts gave in to the flu and canceled. The house had been sold out. Offered the opportunity to fill in for Mr. Watts, Mr. Liu played the program that he would present as a graduation recital at Curtis later the same week. The audience gave Mr. Liu a standing ovation. Mr. Liu later appeared on his own as a recitalist on the same series.

CURTIS
INSTITUTE
WORLD

Curtis lights up the Philadelphia Electric Company building with notice of a world premiere by alumnus/faculty member Ned Rorem (1993).

Pianist, conductor and composer André Previn consults with alumnus/faculty member Ned Rorem on a Rorem score to be played by the Curtis Symphony Orchestra (1993).

the school's preeminent position in years to come. With the successful completion of a three-year, $5.175 million capital campaign announced in 1990, many of the steps toward this plan were made concrete.

In 1997, a Board of Overseers was formed to serve and assist the Board of Trustees in guiding the school in its chartered purpose. Leading this body is Derek Bok, the former president of Harvard University and grandson of Curtis founder Mary Louise Curtis Bok Zimbalist. Another group offering invaluable support is the Friends of Curtis, established in the early 1980s by Rachel Bok Goldman, a granddaughter of Mrs. Bok. Its many efforts include an annual benefit at which significant sums are raised for the Student Assistance Fund. Today some 1,000 households, mostly in the Philadelphia area, are members of the Friends.

Alumni maintain a constantly growing presence at The Institute and in Curtis-related activities in their home cities and countries. In addition to those on the faculty and staff, alumni are represented on the Board of Trustees and the Board of Overseers. In 1995, the first meeting of the Alumni Affairs Council of The Curtis Institute of Music took place. The Council is a vehicle to strengthen ties among alumni worldwide and between alumni and Curtis, for the benefit of current students. It was developed with impetus from Curtis alumni at home and abroad, who saw it as a means of eliciting broader participation from the full Curtis family.

All students who attended Curtis for at least two semesters and who left in good standing are represented by the Alumni Affairs Council. Three organizations are included under the umbrella of the Council. The Curtis Alumni Association West, formed in 1974, has sponsored regional alumni get-togethers as well as master classes. The Alumni Society of Greater Philadelphia presents the popular Alumni Recital Series annually at Curtis Hall, proceeds of which are donated to the school. The Curtis Institute of Music Alumni Association

Flutist James Galway conducts a master class with student Catherine Hays (1994).

(CIMAA), founded in 1974, has hosted the annual "Hoagies in the Square" picnic to welcome new and returning students each fall. In addition to other similar social events, in recent years CIMAA has sponsored several Curtis trumpet master classes. The Alumni Affairs Council hopes to add more groups in the near future.

In 1997, 1998 and 1999, reunions were held over commencement weekend. In 1997, graduates of 1937 and earlier were honored; the following year, graduates of 1938 and of every fifth year after that were recognized. Reminiscences flew during what was described as a forty-eight-hour party, and the reunion has since been decreed an annual event. For the year 2000, all Curtis alumni are invited to participate.

With this kind of support, it is not surprising that The Curtis Institute of Music has been enjoying a period of stability and growth during the last decade-and-a-half, remaining true to its core values and traditions while adjusting realistically to a changing world.

Transformations, Inside and Out

What precisely has been happening behind the doors of those august buildings on Rittenhouse Square?

Perhaps, in fact, one should first consider the doors themselves. In the summer of 1991, the entrance to the main Curtis building was boarded up and painted bright yellow, startling passersby on Locust Street, who were accustomed to a much quieter look on the part of the dignified conservatory. But when the doors reappeared, the heavy oak panels had been replaced by glass. Over the glass was a lacing of iron grillwork, with musical instruments depicted on the door handles. The fanciful design was by the granddaughter of the same Samuel Yellin who had been responsible for many earlier decorative touches within the building, and it is among the last works done by that renowned metalwork factory.

The same year saw other renovations, including the conversion of Studio II-J to a black box theater, used as a large ensemble rehearsal room and as the venue for some master classes, in addition to operatic productions. The work was conceptualized and coordinated by Ralph Batman, administrator of the vocal studies department. In its present form, with black walls and black masonite floor placed over the parquet, the 125-seat theater draws audience attention fully to the stage, inviting intense and intimate participation.

A purchase made four years earlier made possible other much-needed changes. When the English baroque edifice at 1718 Locust Street (contiguous to Knapp Hall) serendipitously came up for sale in 1987, The Institute bought it to house administrative offices, practice rooms and classrooms. These moves, in turn, made it possible to devote all of Knapp Hall

Leonard Slatkin conducts the Curtis Symphony Orchestra.
The soloist is alumna Charlotte Hellekant (1991).

Students Jasmine Lin, on left, and Mu Na in rehearsal with the Curtis Symphony Orchestra (1996).

The Telephone, *by alumnus Gian Carlo Menotti, presented in Curtis Hall with student Heather Dials (1991).*

to the Library. Restoration architect Hyman Myers consulted with The Institute's head librarian, Elizabeth Walker, in planning the renovation, so as to assure that it would allow for up-to-date technology. The Library now has 40% more space, an improved audio/visual department, a special listening room and a new reading room located in an elegant turn-of-the century salon, with display cases for Curtis memorabilia.

Many of the architectural improvements carried out at Curtis over several summers, beginning in 1988, were invisible — new electrical, plumbing, ventilation and heating systems, as well as handicapped-accessible features. Others were of an aesthetic nature, such as the restoration of a nineteenth-century tile floor border by Victorian-era architect Frank Furness, serendipitously uncovered during renovations in the Curtis faculty lounge.

The varied improvements were important, not only because they would provide a safer, more efficient and aesthetically pleasing environment, but because all four Curtis buildings constituted a Philadelphia treasure, having been designated as part of the Philadelphia Register of Historic Places.

What went on inside the newly renovated buildings was, of course, most important. The academic standing of The Curtis Institute of Music was significantly enhanced when, in 1993, it received full accreditation from the Commission on Higher Education of Middle States Association of Colleges and Schools. This assures Curtis students that credit for academic courses taken at the school is transferable and will be accepted, as will a Curtis degree, by all other accredited schools and universities in the United States. It thus pertains both to students who transfer to other schools and those who go on to graduate school.

Another educational effort of significance was a reciprocal agreement signed with the University of Pennsylvania in 1988 and later renewed. This allows qualified Curtis students to enroll, free of charge, in Penn academic courses not offered at The Institute — a dizzying array of subjects, from international law to calculus and oceanography. Composition students at Penn, in turn, gain the opportunity to have new works played by members of the Curtis Orchestra; the reading sessions are audio-taped, with copies sent to the composers. The arrangement has proved extremely valuable to both institutions.

The Penn/Curtis relationship was strengthened in 1998 when The Institute transferred the majority of its Leopold Stokowski Collection to the University's Van Pelt-Dietrich Library. (The instrument collection remains at Curtis.) Included in the gift were original manuscripts, copyrighted transcriptions, recordings, letters, audio and video cassettes, and photographs. At the University, the opportunity for use by scholars and students from around the world is much greater, and the facilities are better suited to the housing and preservation of fragile materials. Penn has developed a multimedia Website for the collection, which enables countless Stokowski fans around the world to learn more about Philadelphia's incomparable maestro.

A Canine Crush

Gary Graffman has had many appreciative listeners, but none more than a puppy who appeared at his feet while he was playing Rachmaninoff's Piano Concerto No. 2 at an outdoor Detroit music festival in 1979. The dog sauntered across the stage and paused at the pianist's feet, sniffing the pedals. Dr. Samuel Ursu, a dentist sitting in the front row, left his seat, tiptoed onstage and led the puppy away while Mr. Graffman played on. After the performance, the dentist shared bows with the musicians.

In 1987, the same Dr. Ursu, who had a particular interest in brass instruments, donated his Piccolo Trumpet to Curtis, with an engraved inscription honoring "Gary Graffman and our mutual friend, the dog." The instrument made its debut at a concert attended by Mr. Graffman and the dentist. The dog had other plans.

Curtis is moving into the next century not only via computers but through courses designed to prepare students for the challenging world that awaits them after graduation. For instance, a course called "The 21st Century Musician," begun in 1994, familiarizes students with a variety of career issues, such as the life of an orchestra musician versus freelancing, the management of medical and legal issues, even the preparation of resumés and publicity photographs. Guest lecturers are nationally recognized leaders in their professions. A seminar for students was held in 1986 on career-related physical and psychological problems of performing artists, and specialists in these fields are available for consultation by students at almost any time.

Increasingly, residents of Philadelphia have come to see The Curtis Institute as a cultural treasure, and the student recitals are now a favorite classical-music destination. Sometimes these prove so popular that overflow audiences must sit in the Common Room where they listen and watch via closed-circuit television. The recitals continue free of charge, on a first-come first-served basis.

Currently, almost one hundred recitals are held each year, sometimes five and even six times per week, with five o'clock concerts added in spring to the customary ones at eight. In any given year, works by about 130 composers are performed. Almost all students perform at least once or twice each semester, and many play several times. Howard Kornblum, a bassoonist by training, ran the student recital series for eighteen years until his death in 1997. His dry wit was appreciated by audiences ("See you again next week — same time, same place, same cost," he would often say at evening's end), though they were not so happy when he chastised them for crinkling their programs, arriving late or sneezing.

Master Teachers, Master Classes

There have been many appointments of note during Mr. Graffman's directorship. Leon Fleisher, himself a student of the great Artur Schnabel, joined the faculty in 1986 and Peter Serkin in 1992. Thoroughly at home in the classical literature, Mr. Serkin is deeply committed to the contemporary as well, having commissioned and performed works by some of today's most eminent composers.

Claude and Pamela Frank, father and daughter, represent a special kind of musical legacy. Pianist Claude Frank, also a former Schnabel student and an acclaimed Beethoven interpreter, joined the Curtis faculty in 1988. His daughter, Pamela, a violinist who maintains an active career both as orchestral soloist and chamber musician, graduated from Curtis one year later and became a faculty member in 1996. Their three joint appearances of father and

Donizetti's L'Elisir d'Amore *is presented by the Curtis Opera Theatre in December 1996.*

Soprano Galina Vishnevskaya, of the Bolshoi Opera, at Curtis for a two-week residency.
Here she works with student Bridgett Hooks (1991).

Violinist Alexander Schneider, formerly of the Budapest String Quartet, visits with director Gary Graffman following a master class (1989).

daughter at Curtis in 1992/93, performing all ten of Beethoven's sonatas for violin and piano, were unforgettable evenings, with crowds gathering at The Institute an hour before the concerts began. (Yo-Yo Ma, who arrived for one of the concerts at a normal time, had to sit on the floor.) The complete sonatas were subsequently recorded by the Franks.

Rafael Druian, who had been concertmaster of both the Cleveland Orchestra and the New York Philharmonic, as well as artist-in-residence at the New England Conservatory of Music, became part of the violin faculty in 1990. Two highly esteemed violinists who have more recently joined the faculty are Victor Danchenko, a graduate of Moscow State Conservatory and a student of David Oistrakh, and the distinguished American artist Ida Kavafian.

Viola study for violinists had not been an option at Curtis for many years, as the esteemed musician Alexander ("Sascha") Schneider discovered while at The Institute to give a master class. Mr. Schneider was so distressed by this lack that he made a substantial donation to restart the program. The first musician to take advantage of the new offering, violinist Choong-Jin Chang, remained at Curtis for two extra years to study viola with alumnus and faculty member Joseph de Pasquale, then principal violist of the Philadelphia Orchestra, after which Mr. Chang joined that orchestra himself as associate principal viola. (In fact, the entire viola section of the Philadelphia Orchestra is heavily weighted with former students of Mr. de Pasquale, who has taught at Curtis since 1964).

Another instrument that has suffered long periods of neglect but, in the early music revival, gained great popularity, is the harpsichord, which has been taught at Curtis since 1988 by Lionel Party.

David Zinman and faculty member Jeffrey Khaner, principal flute of the Philadelphia Orchestra, in rehearsal with the Curtis Symphony Orchestra (1990).

Chamber music has had an increasingly high profile at The Institute, where it is considered an ideal means of teaching young musicians to listen to and respond to other musicians and to improve verbal articulation through the sharing of musical ideas. Gary Graffman, who admits to having come to the field belatedly, through participation at Marlboro in his early twenties, is determined that young instrumentalists leaning toward what he labels the "Paganini-Caprice-and-Double-Stop-Society" will leave Curtis with both enthusiasm and reverence for this form. Thus, more chamber music than ever is required of all instrumentalists, who are asked to form ensembles and to learn specific repertoire each semester. Additionally, instrumental faculty and visiting artists are requested to work with students on chamber music. In 1997, Steven Tenenbom, violist of the Orion String Quartet, became coordinator of the chamber music program. Cellist Peter Wiley added his solo and chamber music expertise when he joined the faculty in 1996.

A group that has risen to international prominence in recent years is the Borromeo String Quartet. Formed by students at Curtis in 1989, the group decided on a permanent partnership after being awarded second prize at the 1990 International String Quartet

Two Curtis alumnae — pianist Cynthia Raim and soprano Benita Valente — present a benefit recital for The Institute (1989).

Serving tea to students is a timeless Curtis tradition, as students violinist Bracha Malkin and clarinetist Anthony McGill know (1999).

Director Gary Graffman and his friend Mickey Mouse (1990).

Competition in Evian. Winning the 1991 Young Concert Artists auditions launched the ensemble, composed of violinists Nicholas Kitchen and Ruggero Allifranchini, violist Hsin-Yun Huang and cellist Yeesun Kim, on an international career.

Another all-Curtis chamber group very active today was formed at the suggestion of John de Lancie, when, after leaving Curtis, he headed a school in Miami. This is the Miami String Quartet, with violinists Ivan Chan and Cathy Meng Robinson, violist Chauncey Patterson and cellist Keith Robinson. They are currently in residence at Lincoln Center in New York and are on the faculty of Florida International University.

The Curtis faculty of master teachers has been supplemented from the beginning by visiting artists and lecturers. Starting in 1987, this aspect of Curtis education was made a more important part of the educational process, both in frequency of appearance and integration into the general curriculum.

In any given year, roughly fifty guest artists appear, each with his or her unique experience. Violinist Igor Oistrakh offered a student helpful advice on the same Kabalevsky violin concerto he himself had rehearsed with the composer. Alumnus composer George Walker interpreted his own brass quintet for a group of students, then lunched with them. Cellist Yo-Yo Ma provided the lower, fundamental tones to accompany the student who was playing a Bach suite for him. And baritone Tom Krause somehow managed to turn himself into the young coquette, Manon, of the Massenet opera, in order to deepen a soprano's understanding of the role.

Visiting artists generally donate their services to the school, or accept a modest honorarium. Gary Graffman was once asked how much a master class by cellist/conductor Mstislav Rostropovich cost Curtis. His answer: a three-pound lobster at the local fish house, Bookbinder's. "And he threw in an Academy of Music concert with the Curtis Orchestra for another lobster and a dozen oysters," added Mr. Graffman. Mr. Rostropovich's teaching relationship with Curtis became more structured in 1990 when he joined the cello faculty, remaining until his National Symphony affiliation ended in 1994 and he returned to his headquarters in Europe.

Other eminent musicians who have joined the faculty since 1986 include harpist (and former Salzedo student) Judy Loman, composer Richard Danielpour, soprano and alumna Marlena Malas and several new members of the Philadelphia Orchestra.

Young Artists Emerge, Losses are Mourned

When a conservatory such as Curtis reaches the three-quarter-century mark, the passing of many great talents is inevitable — even among famously long-lived musicians, kept young through their art. So it was that in recent years several losses were mourned by Curtis through words and, even more fittingly, through music.

On May 8, 1991, Rudolf Serkin died at age eighty-eight at his home in Guilford, Vermont. Remembering him at commencement, Gary Graffman quoted Felix Galimir in saying: "Two words express Rudolf Serkin: music and integrity. Rudi exuded music, and his music exuded integrity."

There were as well several losses among the faculty. On May 22, 1993, Mieczyslaw Horszowski, that great old man of music whose career spanned ninety years and who, seated at the piano, miraculously became young again, died at the age of one hundred. He had taught at Curtis for fifty-one years, inspiring hundreds of students, several of whom continued to work with him until just months before his death. Mr. Horszowski's performances in the final decade of his life were unforgettable. Fortunately, a few recordings — mostly made very late in his life (and, incidentally, recorded in Curtis Hall) — remind us of the man whose musical lineage, from teacher to pupil, can be traced back directly to Mozart.

Coach and accompanist Vladimir ("Billy") Sokoloff, who had a sixty-eight-year involvement with Curtis and who was variously referred to as "The Institute's longest-running attraction," "Dr. Curtis" and "Mr. Piano," died in 1997 at age eighty-four, his passing eased somewhat by the fact that his fellow student and, later, wife, Eleanor Sokoloff, has remained a vital part of the faculty.

That same year saw the death of Jascha Brodsky, first violinist of the Curtis String Quartet and another beloved Curtis presence over many decades. At a memorial concert of Bach and Brahms, violinist Jaime Laredo recalled that Mr. Brodsky had met *his* wife-to-be, violinist Marion Head, while they were both Curtis students. (The link between music and romance has yet to be proved scientifically but is clearly borne out at The Institute.) Violinist

A Mouse Takes Center Stage

September 21, 1990, was officially proclaimed "Fantasia Day" by the City of Philadelphia, in celebration of the fiftieth anniversary and the re-release of the famous Walt Disney film, whose soundtrack was performed by the Philadelphia Orchestra under the direction of Leopold Stokowski. A gala reception, dinner and private showing of the film were held at a local hotel. Curtis had been chosen as the beneficiary for this event because of its long history with Mr. Stokowski.

Unfortunately, during the taking of publicity photographs, Curtis director Gary Graffman was upstaged by an even more famous figure: Mickey Mouse, who had jetted in from Florida, standing five feet, six inches from heels to ears.

Arnold Steinhardt then recounted one of the many stories about Jascha Brodsky, who clearly knew every musician of note in the twentieth century. It seems that Mr. Brodsky, who had just finished his studies with Eugène Ysaÿe, took a boat to America, running into Mischa Elman en route, after which he played a chess game with Sergei Prokofiev and topped off the evening by dining with Sergei Rachmaninoff.

Losses are somewhat balanced by celebrations, and so it is that Curtis marked — through music, of course — key birthdays of composers Lukas Foss, Gian Carlo Menotti, Ned Rorem and George Rochberg, flutist Julius Baker, pianist Eleanor Sokoloff and hornist Mason Jones. Each event was tailored to the individual being honored. Mr. Jones showed up at his party with a shofar in one arm and a waldhorn in the other; he was serenaded with an octet of horns. President/Director Graffman's seventieth birthday was celebrated at the opening orchestral concert of the 1998/99 season with a gala benefit performance and a big party afterward on the stage of the Academy of Music.

In 1989, there was even a 112th birthday celebration, in honor of pianist Isabelle Vengerova. She had died thirty-three years before, but her spirit was fully alive in the more than two dozen former students who gathered in Philadelphia from as far away as Los Angeles, Toronto and Lima, Peru, to dedicate the Vengerova Room, a small studio that had formerly been known as I-F. Among the guests was Mme. Vengerova's nonagenarian nephew and her onetime pupil at St. Petersburg Conservatory, the scholar/author/raconteur Nicolas Slonimsky. Mementos and letters were displayed, including one from Lukas Foss, who said of Mme. Vengerova, "She made me practice. She even made Lenny Bernstein practice. How? She cared so much." Healthy portions of Brahms were followed by a "St. Petersburg Supper" that Mme.Vengerova herself might have served, of borscht, chicken cutlets, kasha and mushrooms.

From Broad and Locust Street to the Swiss Alps

The Symphony Orchestra of The Curtis Institute of Music has maintained its enviable record of success, with alumni occupying almost 25% of the principal desks in the "Big Five" American symphony orchestras, and with almost half of the players in the Philadelphia Orchestra having been trained at Curtis.

While at The Institute, members of the Orchestra participate in at least three public concerts a year, playing regularly at Philadelphia's Academy of Music and on occasion in Carnegie Hall and Alice Tully Hall in New York City, as well as at the Kennedy Center in Washington, D.C. Instrumental study has been facilitated by an increase in the number and quality of school instruments (some generously donated).

Curtis students relax in Rittenhouse Square across from The Institute (1995).

Zubin Mehta rehearses the Curtis Symphony Orchestra (1990).

Alumnus composer Lukas Foss gives a master class as student Tamir Hasson looks on (1999).

Violinist Isaac Stern gives a master class, with student Hsin-Yun Huang paying close attention (1990).

In 1986, one of our day's foremost conducting teachers, Otto-Werner Mueller, was chosen to head the Curtis conducting department. The German-born musician maintains the same post at Juilliard, dividing his time between New York and Philadelphia. Mr. Mueller is known to be a demanding taskmaster, with an "old school" approach that brooks no compromise. Among his favorite responses to a poorly executed phrase: "It is so boring that my socks are falling down!" But he is as kind as he is critical, providing his students regularly with non-musical sustenance in the form of cookies, chocolates and home-baked bread.

Curtis students rehearse twice weekly under Mr. Mueller and faculty member David Hayes, a Curtis graduate who is also music director of the Philadelphia Singers. Mr. Hayes has developed an exchange of ensembles between his two institutions, which has resulted in shared performances of such works as Mahler's Second Symphony, (*Resurrection*), and Sir Michael Tippett's *A Child of Our Time*.

The close relationship that President/Director Graffman formed with leading orchestras around the world during his long career as a soloist has greatly facilitated the tradition of guest conductors at Curtis, both in readings and performance. These continue in impressive number and with endless variety in podium manner: from the formal but inspiring presence of Philadelphia Orchestra music director Wolfgang Sawallisch, who has worked with the students annually at a Saturday morning rehearsal, as Riccardo Muti did before him, to the Russian-born Yuri Temirkanov, who says almost nothing and conveys everything through his facial expressions and arms.

David Zinman, a frequent visitor to Curtis, provides his own special magic. For students of a totally different culture and generation, it is a remarkable experience to learn about such typically American works as Charles Ives' *Three Places in New England* from this veteran conductor. Seated at the podium, he sings, whistles and borrows the concertmaster's violin to illustrate a phrase or two. Recognizing that the students have not been exposed to the America of Ives' time, Mr. Zinman brings that era to vivid life, one minute imitating a pack of coyotes and the next strutting like a marching band. Within the space of one packed rehearsal morning, he conveys every auditory image from ragtime to horse carts.

Some concerts will be long remembered in the annals of Curtis history. In 1987, a half-century after enrolling as a Curtis student, Gary Graffman made his debut with the Orchestra, playing Ravel's Piano Concerto for Left Hand. In 1989, Mstislav Rostropovich, who was then conductor of the National Symphony Orchestra, led a concert that included a work dedicated to him: Leonard Bernstein's *Slava!* (the Russian diminutive of Mstislav as well as a word meaning "glory"). At a post-concert party he received a gift of a Curtis sweatshirt autographed by all hundred-plus orchestra members.

In February 1990, two of the school's most distinguished alumni, Leonard Bernstein and Lukas Foss, were to share the podium at a special concert celebrating the school's

SALZBURG IN PHILADELPHIA

In Salzburg, Austria, Wolfgang Amadeus Mozart's birthplace, there is a central square called Mozartplatz. And now, thanks to The Curtis Institute of Music, there is also a Mozart Place in Philadelphia. In 1991, the bicentennial year of the composer's death, the City of Philadelphia renamed the block-long portion of Bouvier Street that runs north and south between The Institute's four buildings. The new street sign, proclaiming the existence of Mozart Place, was draped in flowers, the Austrian consul was present, and Viennese pastries were served to overflow crowds. At Curtis, a marathon of Mozart's music took place, with faculty and students playing non-stop for four hours.

sixty-fifth anniversary; Mr. Bernstein became ill and Mr. Foss conducted the whole concert. That same year, violinist Isaac Stern celebrated his seventieth birthday with the Curtis Orchestra, playing the Beethoven Violin Concerto first in Philadelphia, then in New York.

On occasion, every aspect of a concert seems Curtis-connected. Such was the case when, in 1998, clarinet graduate and faculty member Anthony Gigliotti was soloist under the baton of another graduate, Robert Spano. The composers represented were, naturally, Curtis products as well: George Rochberg and Ned Rorem.

Among the conductors appearing at Curtis, none is a more vocal and enthusiastic supporter of the school than André Previn, conductor laureate of the London Symphony Orchestra, as well as a highly regarded and versatile composer, jazz pianist and chamber musician. Mr. Previn first conducted at The Institute in 1991. He has since appeared many times with the Curtis Symphony Orchestra in performance, both in New York and Philadelphia.

Mr. Previn also led the Curtis Orchestra in its very first recording, a CD for New World Records of works by Ned Rorem and featuring Gary Graffman as soloist in the Piano Concerto for Left Hand. He also conducted the ensemble on its debut recording for EMI Classics, released in October 1995. The CD, which was produced by Phil Ramone, a key figure in the music entertainment business, includes works of Ralph Vaughan Williams, as well as the world premiere recording of Mr. Previn's own *Reflections*. The CD was critically acclaimed, and listeners obviously felt the same way, because the "New Music" shelf at Tower Records in Center City Philadelphia constantly had to be restocked. Even EMI was surprised when almost all of the CDs that had been pressed were quickly shipped out on order.

When, during the 1998 Christmas season, Mr. Previn was among the artists to be awarded a Kennedy Center Honor for lifetime achievement, the Curtis Symphony Orchestra participated, at his request, on his segment of the CBS telecast.

Performing in Europe has become a custom at Curtis. The Evian connection made during the de Lancie era continued with invitations to the Orchestra for the summers of 1989, 1990 and 1994. It is a major effort to pack and load 8,000 pounds of musical instruments,

Nonagenarian musicologist Nicolas Slonimsky, on left, with Mr. Graffman and violinist Josef Gingold at the 1987 Curtis holiday party.

Giving advice to student John Koen, on right, cellist Yo-Yo Ma conducts a master class (1988).

Pianist Emanuel Ax works with student Stewart Goodyear in a master class (1994).

music and equipment, and to set off across the Atlantic with a passenger list of one hundred-plus musicians. But it is also a rare opportunity for the students to learn the rigors of international musical travel, and an economical venture as well, for the Festival generously covered all expenses, from air fares to room and board, even the cost of visas.

With Mstislav Rostropovich as director of the Festival, the students gave many memorable performances, including the 1990 world premiere of the Schnittke Cello Concerto No. 2, with Mr. Rostropovich as soloist. Story after story is told of the beloved musician, who once gave every Curtis Orchestra member an Evian tee-shirt that he'd personally autographed, presenting each one with a bear hug and a kiss on both cheeks. And who one day, while conducting a rehearsal, placed a small airline bag at his feet on the podium. After a while the bag began to bounce. Without missing a beat, Mr. Rostropovich opened the satchel to let out his tiny dog, who proceeded to jump happily around his master.

In 1998, the setting for a Curtis summer was Verbier, in the Swiss Alps. As the orchestra-in-residence at the festival there, Curtis gave six concerts under such conductors as Kurt Masur and Yuri Temirkanov, with soloists including Maxim Vengerov and Curtis alumnus Yefim Bronfman. Some of the more athletically-inclined students made a habit of a pre-rehearsal mountain climb to get their circulation going, and three of them took on a decidedly offbeat gig: as serenading trumpeters who paraglided down the mountain during opening ceremonies.

Playing it Unsafe

"The Curtis Opera Theatre refuses to play it safe," wrote a local music critic of an unorthodox production of Mozart's *Don Giovanni*, presented by the school.

That description is precisely in keeping with the mission of Mikael Eliasen, who was named head of the vocal studies department in 1989. An internationally noted coach and accompanist, Mr. Eliasen had extensive experience as artistic director of the European Center for Opera and Vocal Arts in Belgium, and, later, as music director of the San Francisco Opera Center. At Curtis, his repertoire is an imaginative blend of contemporary opera, standard works and rarely performed masterpieces. These productions utilize the skills both of Curtis faculty members and outside stage directors and conductors, known for their innovative work on the operatic stage.

Audiences who have come to productions at the school's intimate black box theater, and to larger stages such as the Port of History Museum and Haverford School, have been treated to an array of theatrical events not often available in Philadelphia, including Monteverdi's *The Coronation of Poppea*, Handel's *Alcina*, Tchaikovsky's *Iolanta*, Puccini's *La*

Mstislav Rostropovich conducts a rehearsal at Curtis in preparation for the Evian Festival (1989).

Rondine, Bellini's *I Capuleti e I Montecchi*, Poulenc's *La Voix Humaine* and Copland's *The Tender Land*. The operas are given in staged or semi-staged versions, almost always in the original language, sometimes with the Curtis Symphony Orchestra and at other times with piano or harpsichord accompaniment.

Particularly memorable was *The Emperor of Atlantis*, a one-act opera created in 1944 at the Theresienstadt concentration camp in Czechoslovakia and lost before it had ever been performed. Both the composer, Viktor Ullmann, a student of Schoenberg, and the librettist, Peter Kien, perished during the war, but the score was discovered decades later in a London attic — a symbol of creativity in the face of death. Staged at Curtis in its Philadelphia premiere by Rhoda Levine, who had directed both the world and American premieres, *The Emperor of Atlantis* combined the forces of seven soloists with a chamber orchestra of fourteen.

It is particularly valuable for student composers to see their own works in production at the school. In 1996, Jonathan B. Holland's one-act opera *Naomi in the Living Room* was staged at Curtis with piano accompaniment. Based on a play by Christopher Durang, the opera deals with a dysfunctional family. Rumor has it that another Naomi, Mrs. Graffman, threatened to boycott the production for use — or abuse — of her name, but at last report the two were still friends.

Leading performers sometimes add their own incomparable touches to a work-in-progress. When the Curtis Opera Theatre presented scenes from Tchaikovsky's *Eugene Onegin* in 1991, the renowned Russian soprano and Bolshoi Opera star Galina Vishnevskaya prepared the students during an intensive two-week residency. Having made the role of Tatiana in that opera her own, the raven-haired diva had a wealth of experience on which to draw, holding daily coaching sessions with singers and conductors, during which she guided, cajoled and exhorted the performers from her seat in the Curtis Hall balcony.

Even mishaps have been utilized to the students' advantage. A 1989 performance of Cavalli's *L'Ormindo* was plagued with illness and accidents, but that did not stop the mezzo-soprano with a broken leg from appearing on stage in a knee-high cast. Nor did a bad case of the flu prevent the tenor from appearing (he couldn't sing but mimed his part onstage while two offstage colleagues divided the vocal responsibilities). It all went so well that most of the audience assumed the rather odd staging was intentional.

A cooperative effort with the Opera Company of Philadelphia, formalized in 1994 after some years of an informal collaboration, has provided Curtis students with valuable experience as they prepare to move toward careers in opera. There are two parts to this effort. First, Curtis students make up intern casts for the professional company's productions at the Academy of Music, giving rehearsal readings of complete operas with the Opera Company's orchestra and conductor. Second, Curtis students participate in the development of operas commissioned by the professional company, providing the cast for workshop productions. (Such was the case with Richard Wargo's *Ballymore*, an opera based upon a Brian Friel play.) A number of students introduced to the Opera Company of Philadelphia in this fashion were subsequently engaged by its management.

Although over 300 aspirants audition for Mr. Eliasen each year, the enrollment remains limited to about twenty-five students so as to allow for individual attention. One unique aspect of the vocal studies department is that students are free to ask for a specific (adjunct) teacher, with approval of Mr. Eliasen.

Since Curtis' founding, over forty students have sung with the Metropolitan Opera Company. Recent graduates Charlotte Hellekant, mezzo-soprano, Michael Schade and Thomas Studebaker, tenors, Kamel Boutros, baritone, and Kevin Short, bass-baritone, are among them.

Approaching the 21st Century

Every year in February and March, young applicants descend upon The Curtis Institute of Music, hoping to be among the favored who are accepted as students. Sitting, standing, pacing in the Common Room, they wait to be called to the audition room. The process is extremely rigorous, with only about six percent of those who apply accepted.

Remarkably, according to long-time observers like cellist Orlando Cole, who has been intimately connected with Curtis over its lifetime, the quality of entering students today is as high as that of graduating students seventy-five years ago. What makes acceptance at Curtis even more difficult is that auditions are held only for disciplines that have openings. (In the case of the tuba, there is space for just one student, with a vacancy occurring about every four years.) The course of study at Curtis remains open-ended, with readiness for graduation determined by the major teacher. The total student body is usually around 165, just enough to maintain a full orchestra and opera department, with a small added number of keyboard players, as well as conducting and composition students. The student/faculty ratio remains an intensive two-to-one.

Curtis has become ever more international in student body, with the scales having tipped for the first time in favor of foreign students during the 1995/96 academic year. They come from all over the world: Argentina and Belarus, China and Lithuania, Singapore and South Africa, Canada and Mexico. One might wonder how so diverse a mix of ages and backgrounds could ever relate to each other. Yet those who have attended the week-long orientation sessions that initiate each school year know that by the time of the traditional fall picnic in Rittenhouse Square, bonding has already started.

Billy to the Rescue

During one of the Curtis Symphony Orchestra's several trips to the Evian Festival in France, Maestro Rostropovich was rehearsing a new work by Ned Rorem. There was to be a short piano solo, but the pianist of the Orchestra (who shall remain nameless) had overslept and the piano bench was vacant. Just before the solo, a raffish-looking fellow, dressed like a French workman, strode from the rear of the auditorium onto the stage. Mr. Rostropovich glanced at him and continued to conduct with an expression of some apprehension. The "workman" plopped onto the piano bench, squinted at the new music, and, exactly on cue, played as if he'd been rehearsing for weeks. He was, of course, Vladimir Sokoloff.

Graduation, although sometimes bittersweet, is a time for celebration. Pictured, left to right, are Valérie Muzzolini, Sarah Hatsuko Hicks and Margo Tatgenhorst (1999).

By the three-quarter century mark, the illustrious line of Curtis graduates totals some 3,500. Proportionately, The Institute continues to produce the largest body of notable musicians of any conservatory in the world.

Gary Graffman is sometimes asked how The Curtis Institute of Music has changed during his leadership. His response: "Not at all, I hope!" It is true, he says, that there have been some "enhancements" — that is, adjustments to the curriculum and to daily life and to governance, all of which recognize the realities of the day. But changes in basic philosophy would be unnecessary, unwise, and, Mr. Graffman believes, unthinkable.

"In an increasingly homogenized world," says the head of Curtis, "The Institute has stubbornly maintained its own decidedly individualistic (if slightly eccentric) profile. As a result, the school is sometimes labeled as conservative, elitist, insular, paternalistic — even anachronistic. Nevertheless, or perhaps because of these qualities, Curtis has produced an astonishing number of this century's most distinguished musicians. And this is without even taking into account its small size. If something is working so well, why change it?"

Thus, as The Curtis Institute of Music celebrates its seventy-fifth year, Mr. Graffman sees its challenge as being how *not* to change, how to maintain without compromise the artistic ideals and musical standards that Mary Louise Curtis Bok, Leopold Stokowski and Josef Hofmann espoused when the doors first opened in 1924.

The unbroken record of success that has been achieved at The Curtis Institute of Music has proved the validity of their concept. "Castle-building in Spain," as Mrs. Bok once called it, was at first only a dream. Today it is an enduring reality.

The Bok Room with Mary Louise Curtis Bok Zimbalist looking down from her portrait on a scene of laughter, conversation and music-making. Students, left to right, are Randall Gregoire, Heather Conner, Timothy Fain, Arash Amini and Jasmine Lin (1997).

APPENDIX I

The Curtis Institute of Music Graduation 1934–1999

	Commencement Speakers	Honorary Degrees
1934	Thomas Sovereign Gates Wladyslaw Sokolowski	Leopold Godowsky Marcella Sembrich
1935	——	Wiktor Labunski
1936	——	——
1937	——	——
1938	——	——
1939	The Right Reverend Joseph M. Corrigan	——
1940	Walter Damrosch	——
1941	The Reverend Joseph Fort Newton	Frederick E. Hahn
1942	Frank Aydelotte	——
1943	Curtis Bok	Sidney Homer
1944	——	——
1945	Samuel Barber	Samuel Barber Gian Carlo Menotti
1946	The Reverend Frederick R. Griffin	Eugene Ormandy Rosario Scalero
1947	——	——
1948	Olin Downes	——
1949	Harold E. Stassen	Carlos Salzedo Isabelle Vengerova
1950	Henry S. Drinker	John N. Burk
1951	Owen J. Roberts	Rudolf Serkin
1952	Gerald F. Flood	Alexander Hilsberg William Kincaid Alexander McCurdy, Jr. Marcel Tabuteau
1953	Virgil Thomson	——
1954	Catherine Drinker Bowen	Ivan Galamian
1955	Carleton Sprague Smith	——
1956	Paul Henry Lang	——
1957	Nellie Lee Bok	Edith Evans Braun Vittorio Giannini Constant Vauclain
1958	Curtis Bok	——
1959	Alfred Williams	Vladimir Sokoloff
1960	Polycarp Kusch	Lea Luboshutz
1961	Loren C. Eiseley	——
1962	George P. Orr	——
1963	Samuel Barber	——
1964	I. M. Levitt	——
1965	Gian Carlo Menotti	Leo Rosenek
1966	Robert W. Neathery	——
1967	Donald Barnhouse	——
1968	Gian Carlo Menotti	——
1969	Richard F. Sterba, M.D.	Mieczyslaw Horszowski Sol Schoenbach
1970	——	Pablo Casals
1971	Frederick Dorian	——
1972	Willo von Moltke	Mstislav Rostropovich Max Rudolf
1973	Sir Ernst Gombrich	——
1974	M. Todd Cooke	——
1975	Ralph Ellison	Efrem Zimbalist
1976	Romaldo Giurgola	——
1977	Henry Pleasants	Henry Pleasants
1978	George Rochberg	——
1979	David P. Eastburn	——
1980	Philip Nelson	John de Lancie
1981	Max Rudolf	Marian Anderson
1982	Ned Rorem	Ned Rorem
1983	Gian Carlo Menotti	Mrs. Cary W. Bok Mrs. Curtis Bok
1984	Boris Goldovsky	——
1985	Todd Duncan	Todd Duncan
1986	George Rochberg	Jascha Brodsky Orlando Cole
1987	Schuyler Chapin	——
1988	Betty Allen	Lukas Foss George Rochberg
1989	Isaac Stern	Isaac Stern
1990	Joseph W. Polisi	Joseph W. Polisi
1991	Riccardo Muti	Riccardo Muti
1992	Edward G. Rendell	Edward G. Rendell
1993	Sheldon Hackney	Sheldon Hackney
1994	Wolfgang Sawallisch	Wolfgang Sawallisch
1995	André Previn	André Previn
1996	Kitty Carlisle Hart	Kitty Carlisle Hart
1997	Derek Bok	Derek Bok George Walker
1998	Anne d'Harnoncourt	Herbert Axelrod Anne d'Harnoncourt
1999	Ned Rorem	——

Appendix II

The Curtis Institute of Music Faculty 1924–1999

Name	Subject	Years
Adler, Lawrence	Head of Academic Department	1924–26
Adonaylo, Raquel	Voice, Vocal Repertoire	1975–90
Aguilar, Karen Mary, Ph.D.	English Literature and Composition	1972–77
Aldrich, Perley Dunn	Voice	1924–25
Aldwell, Edward	Musical Studies	1971–
Allen, Betty	Voice	1988–90
Alwyne, Hora	History of Music	1926–28
Aronoff, Max	Viola	1929–43; 1956–81
Ashbaker, Susan Shiplett	Opera & Voice Coach	1993–
Auer, Leopold	Violin	1928–30
Auker, Hazel	Tutor	1961–66
Bachmann, Edwin	Violin	1928–32
Backhaus, Wilhelm	Piano	1925–26
Bailly, Louis	Viola, Chamber Music	1925–41
Baker, Julius	Flute	1980–
Baker, Robert	Make-up	1976–77
Bally, Georges	French	1926–27
Barad, Michael	Tutor	1973–74
Barber, Samuel	Supplementary Piano Madrigal Chorus Composition	1931–33 1939–42 1965–71
Barclay, Dagmar Rybner	Vocal Coach	1925–33
Barclay, John	Vocal Coach, English Diction	1931–32
Battin, Isaac L.	Acoustics	1926–27
Bayani, Yousef	Tutor	1976–77
Bazell, Marciem	Make-up	1984–
Beck, Jean B., Ph.D.	French, History of Music	1924–38
Behrend, Jeanne	Supplementary Piano	1936–43
Bellamann, Henry	Dean	1931–32
Bengtsson, Erling	Violoncello	1951–53
Berkowitz, Ralph	Accompanist	1937–43
Bert, Berthe	Piano	1924–25
Bilger, David	Trumpet	1997–
Bimboni, Alberto	Opera Coach	1929–33; 1936–38
Blatter, Alfred	Acoustics, Computers, Orchestration	1989–
Bloom, Myron	Horn	1982–
Bly, Edith Wells	Supplementary Piano	1926–27
Boeckmans, Marcel H.	Fencing	1929–30
Bolet, Jorge	Supplementary Piano Piano, Head of Department	1939–42 1977–86
Bollinger, Blair	Bass Trombone	1997–
Bolotine, Leonid	Violin	1929–30
Bonade, Daniel	Clarinet	1924–28; 1931–33; 1940–42
Bonamore-Graves, Alessandra	Italian	1981–94
Bonelli, Richard	Voice	1941–43; 1950–55
Bookspan, Michael	Orchestral Repertoire (Percussion) Timpani and Percussion	1980– 1987–
Bourdin-Bacher, Marie	French	1926–28
Boyd, Morrison	History of Music	1924–25
Boyle, George	Piano	1924–26
Boyle, Pearl	Supplementary Piano	1924–26
Braun, Edith Evans	Elements of Music	1942–69
Brecht, Harold	Elementary French	1964–65
Brees, Anton	Campanology	1929–33
Britt, Horace	Violoncello	1924–25
Brodsky, Jascha	Violin, Chamber Music	1932–33; 1941–42; 1955–97
Brodsky, Vera	Two-Piano Repertoire	1937–38
Brunyate, Roger	Acting, Stage Directing Head of Opera Department Dramatic Coach	1987–88 1988–89 1989–90
Buchman, Carl	Coach	1936–38
Burch, Maureen	Secondary School Division	1977–83
Burkhardt, Theodore W.	Acoustics	1987–88
Cahier, Mme. Charles	Voice	1924–27
Cailliet, Lucien	Clarinet	1928–30
Caporello, Corradina	Italian Diction	1995–
Carlyss, Gerald	Percussion	1968–87
Carol, Norman	Orchestral Repertoire (Strings)	1979–
Carrigan, Michael D.	Secondary School Division History	1981–83 1982–84
Casiello, Marianne	Voice	1974–90
Caston, Saul	Trumpet	1924–42
Catudal, Jacques	Introduction to Philosophy, Aesthetics	1993–
Cerone, David	Violin	1975–85
Chambers, James	Horn	1943–46
Chasins, Abram	Supplementary Piano	1926–34
Chilkovsky, Nadia	Eurythmics	1946–68
Chinatti, Luigi	Italian Diction	1976–77
Chotzinoff, Samuel	Music Criticism	1937–40
Cohen, Isidore	Chamber Music	1974–77
Cole, Orlando	Violoncello Chamber Music	1933–34; 1939–42; 1953– 1986–
Colucci, Matthew, Ph.D.	Theory	1959–71
Conn, Therese F.	Tutor, Secondary School Division English Literature and Composition	1977–83 1983–86
Connell, Horatio	Voice	1924–33
Connelly, Lawrence	Tutor	1974–76
Conner, Wayne	History of Opera, History of Singing	1985–
Conradi, Austin	Piano	1924–25
Corwin, Marion	Tutor	1955–61
Coryell, Marian	Supplementary Piano	1927–32

Name	Subject	Years
Costello, Marilyn	Harp	1961–98
Cowart, Robert	Diction	1992–95
Cox, Mary Anthony	Theory	1969–74
Crittenden, Richard	Stage Director	1977–87
Cuckson, Robert	Musical Studies	1991–
Dalley, John	Chamber Music	1968–71
Danchenko, Victor	Violin	1994–
Danielpour, Richard	Composition	1997–
Danner, Dorothy	Stagecraft	1990–96
Daudon, René J.	French	1929–38; 1957–64
Deak, Stephen	Violoncello	1929–32
de Bros, Esther	German Diction	1973–77
de Gogorza, Emilio	Voice	1925–40
de Lancie, John	Oboe, Chamber Music (Woodwinds) Director, The Curtis Institute of Music Orchestral Repertoire (Woodwinds)	1954–85 1977–85 1979–85
de Montoliu, Placido	Eurythmics, Platform Deportment Spanish, Italian	1925–40 1933–40
de Pasquale, Joseph	Viola	1964–
de Santis, Louis	Clarinet	1930–31
del Negro, Ferdinand	Bassoon, Contrabassoon	1928–39; 1944–46
Di Blasi, Maria Rota	Italian	1971–81
Di Blasi, Sebastiano, Ph.D.	Italian	1958–72
Diller, Angela	Theory	1924–25
Dippel, Andreas	Operatic Training	1924–25
Dodson, Glenn	Trombone Chamber Music (Brass)	1969–98 1975–98
Donatelli, Philip	Tuba	1928–42
Dorian, Frederick	Music History	1975–77
Douty, Nicholas	Oratorio and Repertoire	1924–25
Drew, James J.	Acoustics	1983–87
Druian, Phyllis Rugg	Librarian	1942–47
Druian, Rafael	Violin	1990–
Drummond, Ethel S.	Theory, Supplementary Piano	1924–33
Duncan, Todd	Voice	1977–90
Ealer, Sarah Jane	Tutor	1952–56
Eastman, Katherine	English	1929–30
Effron, David	Opera Orchestra Coach, Principal Conductor	1970–76 1973–77 1976–77
Eliasen, Mikael	Coach Director of Musical Studies (Vocal) Head of Vocal Studies	1986– 1988–89 1989–
Elster-Mercurio, Barbara	Movement and Dance	1989–90
Emgarth, Annette H.	French	1965–66
Englander, Lester	French	1937–41
Estreich, George	Introduction to Drama	1992–93
Eto, Reiko	Accompanist	1959–60

Name	Subject	Years
Eto, Toshiya	Violin, String Ensemble	1953–61
Farnam, Lynnwood	Organ	1927–30
Fernberger, Samuel	Psychology	1926–32
Feuermann, Emanuel	Violoncello	1941–42
Field, Eleanor	Tutor	1939–41
Fields, Eleanor	Supplementary Piano	1926–28
Fink, Myron	Theory, Composition	1970–73; 1974–76
Finn, Caesar	Applied Aesthetics	1931–32
Fitzpatrick, Eleanor	Tutor	1951–66
Fitzpatrick, Robert	Orchestra, Executive Assistant to the Director Dean	1980–85 1986–
Flagello, Nicholas	Composition	1964–65
Fleisher, Leon	Piano	1986–
Flesch, Carl	Violin	1924–28
Fonaroff, Vera	Violin	1929–33
Frank, Claude	Piano	1988–
Frank, Pamela	Violin	1996–
Frantz, Clair	Tutor Secondary School Division, Head of Department	1976–78 1978–81
Frantz, Florence	Assistant in Piano	1930–33
Freschl, Marion Szekeley	Voice	1945–50
Fugmann, Andreas	Opera Coach	1932–33
Fulton, Thomas	Opera	1973–76
Galamian, Ivan	Violin	1944–81
Galimir, Felix	Chamber Music (Strings and Mixed Ensembles), Head of Department Violin	1972– 1992–
Gardiner, Walter	Tutor	1951–52
Garfield, Bernard	Bassoon	1975–80; 1985–
Gari, Giulio	Voice	1970–75
Gaujot, Marguerite	French	1954–55
Gerassi, Stepha	German, Russian, Russian Literature	1969–76
Gerhard, Charles	Trombone	1931–42
Germani, Fernando	Organ	1931–33
Gerson, Robert	English Diction	1951–52
Giannini, Vittorio	Composition	1956–64
Gigliotti, Anthony	Clarinet Chamber Music (Woodwinds)	1951–80 1977–80; 1985–
Gittelson, Frank	Violin	1924–27
Glandorf, Matthew	Musical Studies	1995–
Goldberg, Szymon	Violin	1981–93
Goldovsky, Boris	Opera Coach Head of Opera Department Operatic Techniques	1931–37 1977–85 1980–83
Goodman, Thomas	History of Art	1983–90
Gotlobe, Jack L.	Librarian	1954–61

Name	Subject	Years
Graf, Herbert	Opera	1950–60
Graffman, Gary	Piano Director, The Curtis Institute of Music President/Director, The Curtis Institute of Music	1980– 1986–95 1995–
Gregoretti, Anna	Italian Diction	1973–76
Gregory, Euphemia Giannini	Voice, Italian Diction	1927–73
Grolle, Johann	Director, The Curtis Institute of Music	1924–25
Grooters, Robert	English Diction, German Diction	1981–93
Grubb, Thomas	French Diction, Vocal Repertoire	1970–77
Grupp, David	Percussion	1950–53
Guenther, Sara Elizabeth	Tutor Secondary School Division	1976–77 1978–83
Guetter, Walter	Bassoon	1925–32
Gusikoff, Charles	Trombone, Brass Ensemble	1947–66
Guth, Otto	Opera Coach	1973–77
Hadley, Katharine	Tutor	1958–66
Hageman, Richard	Vocal Coach	1925–29
Hagen, Daron	Composition Seminar for Non-Majors	1996–98
Hamer, Janice	Musical Studies	1996–
Harbeson, William Page	English Composition, Literature, Poetry	1925–33
Harley, Katharine	Tutor	1952–55
Harms, William	Supplementary Piano	1931–40
Haroz, Nitzan	Trombone	1998–
Harris, Stephen B.	Tutor	1969–73
Harrison, James	Theory	1970–72
Harshaw, Margaret	Voice, Opera	1970–77
Hart, Deborah	Tutor	1974–76
Hartman, Elizabeth R.	Librarian	1947–54
Hartzer, Richard	Violin	1925–28
Haslam, Elizabeth L.	English Composition, Literature	1986–91
Hawrysz, Ilse	German German Diction	1978– 1986–
Hayden, Mary-Jean B.	English as a Second Language	1986–
Hayes, David	Elements of Conducting Orchestra, Staff Conductor	1990– 1992–
Head, Marion	Violin	1939–42
Heifetz, Ruvin	Violin	1936–38
Helmer, Eugene	Accompanist	1937–40
Henry, Barbara D.	Head Librarian	1973–75
Herman, Alice	Chinese Literature	1991–92
Hettinger, Sarah	Librarian	1935–42
Higdon, Jennifer	Musical Studies	1994–
Hilsberg, Alexander	Violin, Conductor of Orchestra	1930–53
Hinger, Fred	Percussion	1953–68
Hires, William L.	History Dean of Academic Studies	1981–82 1982–87
Hodge, Muriel	Supplementary Piano	1927–28
Hofmann, Josef	Piano Director, The Curtis Institute of Music	1924–38 1927–38

Name	Subject	Years
Hoiby, Lee	Theory	1950–52
Hollingsworth, Stanley	Theory, Solfège, Opera Coach	1949–55
Horner, Anton	Horn	1924–42
Horszowski, Mieczyslaw	Piano	1942–93
Irons, Diedre	Supplementary Piano	1969–77
Jaber, Thomas I.	Opera Department Accompanying, Coach, Vocal Repertoire	1977–88
Jacobinoff, Sascha	Violin	1924–27
Jaffe, Charles	Chamber Music	1941–42
Jerome, Wilbert	Music History	1976–77
Johnson, Gilbert D.	Trumpet Chamber Music (Brass)	1969–75 1973–75
Jones, Mason	Horn, Brass Ensemble Orchestral Repertoire Chamber Music (Woodwinds)	1946–82 1979–95 1985–95
Kaderabek, Frank	Trumpet	1975–
Kaufman, Harry	Accompanying	1924–41
Kavafian, Ida	Violin	1998–
Khaner, Jeffrey	Flute Chamber Music (Woodwinds)	1985– 1992–
Kimmel, Merl F.	History	1984–
Kincaid, William	Flute, Woodwind Ensemble	1924–67
King, Gordon C.	English	1925–26
King, Samuel Arthur	Platform Deportment, English Diction	1924–32
Klar, Audrey	Theory	1978–82
Klarmann, Adolf, Ph.D.	Great Books	1958–61
Koh, Eunae	Opera Department, Staff Pianist	1997–
Kohler, Sandra	English Literature	1991–92
Kormi, Iraj	Tutor	1973–76
Kovar, Simon	Bassoon	1939–42
Krause, Katherine C.	Tutor	1969–70
Krauss, Samuel	Trumpet	1947–68
Krell, John	Flute	1967–71; 1980–85
Krzywicki, Paul	Tuba	1972–
Kullman, Charles	Voice	1971–72
Lallerstedt, Ford	Musical Studies Chair of Musical Studies Department	1973– 1994–
Lambert, Alexander	Piano	1928–30
Landis, Joan Hutton, Ph.D.	English Literature Chair of Liberal Arts Department	1977– 1987–
Landowska, Wanda	Harpsichord, Lecturer	1925–28
Laredo, Jaime	Violin	1971–
Lawrence, Lucile	Harp	1927–33
Lee, Sylvia	Vocal Repertoire and Interpretation	1970–90
Lenrow, Elbert	English	1926–32
Lert, Ernst Joseph Maria, Ph.D.	Operatic Acting	1936–38
Levin, Robert D.	Theory	1968–73
Levin, Sylvan	Opera Coaching, Accompanying, Assistant Conductor Repertory Coach	1929–39 1977–78

Name	Subject	Years
Levine, Joseph	Supplementary Piano, Opera Class Accompanist	1932–41
Levine, Rhoda	Opera and Drama, Dance Stagecraft/Acting	1970–75 1990–
Lewis, Richard	Voice	1968–71
Li, Jian	Supplementary Piano, Staff Pianist	1995–
Liebling, Estelle	Voice	1937–38
Lipkin, Seymour	Piano	1969–
Littlefield, Catherine	Dancing	1930–31
Liu, Meng–Chieh	Staff Pianist	1993–
Liuzzi, Don	Timpani and Percussion	1994–
Loeb, David	Musical Studies Composition	1973–95 1981–
Lofton, David	Vocal Repertoire, Coach	1984–94
Loman, Judy	Harp	1998–
Longy, Renée	Solfège	1926–41
Lotz, Paul	Trombone	1925–26
Luboshutz, Lea	Violin	1927–47
Ludwig, Elizabeth S.	Tutor	1969–73
Luvisi, Lee	Piano	1956–62
Macatsoris, Chris	Opera Department, Coach	1970–78
Makanowitzky, Paul	Violin	1965–71
Malas, Marlena Kleinman	Voice	1986–
Malensek, Ben	Vocal Repertoire, Coach	1988–91
Mann, Alfred	Recorder	1939–41
Mann, Robert	Violin	1997–99
Mapes, Gordon	Special Services Librarian Head Librarian	1955–61 1961–73
Mario, Queena	Voice	1931–33
Martin, Louis	Theory	1969–73
Martinů, Bohuslav	Composition	1955–56
Masséna, Martha Halbwachs	Supplementary Piano	1927–40; 1946–85
	Vocal Repertoire	1978–85
Mauclair, Blanche	French	1954–57
Mayo, Elton B., M.D.	Psychology	1924–26
McCurdy, Alexander	Organ	1935–72
McGinn, Jeanne M.	English Literature	1994–
McGinnis, Robert	Clarinet	1934–40
McLane, Ralph	Clarinet	1947–51
McLaughlin, Nancy	Tutor	1951–53
Meiff, Albert	Violin	1928–32
Menendez, Louis	Opera Department, Staff Pianist	1988–94
Meng, Mei-Mei	Musical Studies	1982–
Menotti, Gian Carlo	Composition, Dramatic Forms	1941–55; 1965–71
Meredith, Eleanor	Solfège	1930–33
Mertens, Georges	Opera Coach	1931–32
Micahnik, Richard	Fencing	1976–77

Name	Subject	Years
Milanov, Zinka	Voice	1977–81
Miller, Frank	Violoncello Class	1932–33
Minsker, John	Chamber Music (Woodwinds)	1979–85
Mitchell, Ercelle	Supplementary Piano	1927–28
Mlynarski, Emil	Orchestra and Conducting Class	1929–31
Moiseiwitsch, Benno	Piano	1926–27
Montanaro, Donald	Clarinet Chamber Music (Woodwinds)	1980– 1981–
Morris, Reginald O.	Composition, Theory	1926–28
Morrisett, James S.	Supplementary Piano	1926–27
Motten, Louise	Tutor	1957–59
Mueller, Otto-Werner	Conducting, Head of Department; Orchestra	1986–
Munz, Mieczyslaw	Piano	1930–32; 1941–42
Murphy, Joseph M.	History of Music	1979–80
Nazarevitsch, Xenia	Supplementary Piano	1925–32
Needleman, William	Theory	1976–78
Nichols, Roy F., Ph.D.	World History	1925–32
Nolan, Patrick J.	English Composition	1970–71
Norden, Lindsay	Theory	1924–26
Norris, John	Acting	1995–99
Nowicki, Susan	Opera & Voice Coach	1987–
Orlando, Danielle	Assistant to Head of Opera Department, Coach Principal Opera Coach	1986–88 1988–
Ormandy, Eugene	Orchestra	1968–77
Padow, Phyllis	Tutor	1973–76
Paget, Ethel M.	Supplementary Piano	1927–32
Panitz, Murray W.	Flute	1969–80
Parme, Fred	Saxophone	1926–27
Party, Lionel	Harpsichord	1988–
Pastor, Freda	Supplementary Piano	1936–90
Patenaude-Yarnell, Joan	Voice	1996–
Pavicic, Nick J.	Tutor	1970–73
Péchin, Marguerite	French	1954–64
Penha, Michel	Violoncello	1924–25
Pennington, Martha	Tutor	1976–77
Perndorfer, Ingeborg	German	1976–77
Petit, Annie	Musical Studies Supplementary Piano	1974–76 1976–
Piatigorsky, Gregor	Violoncello	1942–51
Pons, Max	Coach	1928–38
Popper, Felix	Opera Department, Coach	1974–77
Popper, Fredric	Assistant to Head of Opera Department, Coach Operatic Techniques	1977–86 1980–83
Portnoy, Bernard	Clarinet	1943–47
Poyner, Margaret	Supplementary Voice Voice	1990– 1992–97

Name	Subject	Years
Press, Michael	Violin	1924–25
Primrose, William	Viola, Chamber Music	1942–51
Puppin, Carla	Art History	1991–
Rachlin, Ezra	Supplementary Piano	1936–37; 1939–41
Rantz, Jock	English Diction	1946–50
Rawson, Therese Casadesus	French, French Diction Humanities Head of Modern Language Studies	1969– 1987–93 1987–
Reimesch, Ilsa	Accompanist and Coach	1927–30
Reiner, Fritz	Orchestra, Conducting Class	1931–41
Reisenberg, Nadia	Supplementary Piano	1934–38
Resnikoff, Vera	Supplementary Piano	1925–32; 1938–40
Reynolds, Veda	Violin	1942–61
Rich, Martin	Coach	1947–50
Rich, Thaddeus	Assistant Conductor of Orchestra	1925–26
Riedel, Karl	Opera Coach	1930–32
Robinor, Genia	Accompanist	1938–41
Robinson, Harold Hall	Double Bass	1995–
Rochberg, George	Form and Analysis	1947–54
Rodzinski, Artur	Orchestra and Conducting Class	1926–29
Romani, Gabriella	Italian	1994–
Rorem, Ned	Composition	1980–
Rosand, Aaron	Violin	1981–
Rose, Jonathan E.	History	1980–81
Rose, Leonard	Violoncello	1936–63
Rosenek, Leo	Vocal Coach	1938–65
Rosenfeld, Natania	English Language and Literature	1992–94
Rosenthal, Moriz	Piano	1926–28
Ross, James	Elements of Conducting	1989–90
Rostropovich, Mstislav	Violoncello	1990–95
Rubanoff, Joseph	Vocal Coach	1929–32
Rudolf, Max	Opera and Orchestra Conducting	1970–73 1983–86
Ruhrseitz, Esther	Voice, Vocal Coach	1925–27
Ruhrseitz, Kurt	Vocal Coach	1925–26
Rulau, Ellen	Voice	1970–75
Rupp, Franz	Vocal Coach, Vocal Repertoire	1968–72
St. Pierre, Donald	Opera & Voice Coach	1990–
Salmond, Felix	Violoncello	1925–43
Salzedo, Carlos	Harp	1924–61
Saperton, David	Piano	1924–41
Sataloff, Robert, M.D.	Voice Science Seminar	1987–94
Sato, Keiko	Supplementary Piano	1987–
Saumelle, Minna	Special Diction for Singers	1925–31
Scalero, Rosario	Composition	1924–33; 1935–46
Schneider, Mischa	Chamber Music	1970–85

Name	Subject	Years
Schoenbach, Peter J., Ph.D.	Dean Portuguese, Spanish, 20th Century Latin American Literature	1973–77 1974–77
Schoenbach, Sol	Bassoon Chamber Music (Woodwinds)	1943–44; 1946–77; 1980–85 1974–77; 1981–85
Schorr, Friedrich	Voice	1943–45
Schulman, Leonard	Percussion	1947–50
Schumann, Elisabeth	Voice	1937–47
Schwar, Oscar	Timpani	1925–42
Scott, Kathleen	Coach	1981–86
Scott, Roger	Double Bass	1948–97
Scott, Yumi Ninomiya	Violin	1970–
Seiver, Lawrence	Tutor	1970–73
Sembrich, Marcella	Voice	1924–32
Serkin, Peter	Piano	1992–
Serkin, Rudolf	Piano Director, The Curtis Institute of Music	1939–76 1968–76
Shaffer, Esther	Tutor	1930–31
Sharlip, Benjamin	Chamber Music Coach	1932–34
Shepherd-Barr, Kirsten	English Literature	1995–96
Shryock, Richard	World History	1924–25
Shumsky, Oscar	Violin	1961–65
Shumway, Mary Q., Ph.D.	German	1930–69
Siena, Daniela	Italian Diction	1970–73
Silverstein, Barbara	Opera Department, Musical Assistant	1976–77
Simons, Gardell	Trombone	1924–30
Singher, Margareta	French Grammar and Diction	1962–63; 1965–67
Singher, Martial	Voice, Opera	1955–68
Smith, Henry Charles	Trombone, Tuba, Brass Ensemble	1966–67
Smith, Joy Pottle	Supplementary Piano	1969–70
Smith, Lawrence L.	Opera Department	1969–70
Smith, Mark Russell	Elements of Conducting	1987–89
Smith, William R.	Orchestra	1953–93
Soffray, Anne-Marie	Theory, Solfège	1928–32; 1935–56
Sokoloff, Eleanor	Supplementary Piano Piano	1936–49 1949–
Sokoloff, Vladimir	Vocal Repertoire, Chamber Music, Director of Concert Programs, Head of Accompaniment	1938–94
Soyer, David	Violoncello Chamber Music	1968– 1974–78
Spofford, Grace H.	Dean	1925–31
Steinhardt, Arnold	Chamber Music Violin	1968–78 1972–
Stewart, M. Dee	Trombone	1967–80
Stewart, Mrs. Wood	Voice	1924–25

Name	Subject	Years
Stöhr, Richard	Theory	1939–41
Stokowski, Leopold	Orchestra	1924–27
Strasfogel, Ignace	Head of Opera Department	1986–88
Stroumillo, Olga	Piano Assistant to Mme. Vengerova	1956–57
Sullivan, Anne	Musical Studies	1982–
Summers, Helen	English	1928–31
Sumsion, Herbert	Theory	1926–28
Sung, Hugh	Staff Pianist Director of Instrumental Accompaniment	1993– 1996–
Suppa, Carl M.	Dean of Students	1985–86
Svécenski, Claire	Supplementary Piano	1928–32
Svécenski, Louis	Chamber Music	1924–27
Symonette, Lys Bert	Coach, Vocal Repertoire, German, German Diction	1975–85
Szewczyk, David M.	History	1976–77; 1978–79
Tabuteau, Louise André	French Grammar and Diction	1938–54
Tabuteau, Marcel	Oboe, Woodwind Ensemble	1925–42; 1943–54
Taylor, Deems	Composition	1925–26
Tenenbom, Steven	Chamber Music (Strings)	1996–
Terranova, Elaine	English Literature	1998–
Thompson, Oscar	Professional Criticism	1931–32
Thompson, Randall	Orchestration Director, The Curtis Institute of Music	1939–41 1939–41
Torello, Anton	Double Bass	1926–42; 1947–48
Torello, Carl	Double Bass	1943–47
Tree, Michael	Chamber Music Viola	1968–78 1972–
Trepel, Shirley	Violoncello	1946–49
Triggs, Harold	Two-Piano Repertoire	1937–38
Türk, Martha	German	1931–41
Tuttle, Karen	Viola	1945–55; 1986–
	Chamber Music (Strings and Mixed Ensembles)	1978–
Uris, Dorothy	English Diction	1976–77
van Emden, Harriet	Voice	1926–36
Van Witsen, Leo	Make-up, Costuming	1977–86
Vauclain, Constant	Theory, Composition	1939–63
Vengerova, Isabelle	Piano	1924–56
Vernon, Charles	Trombone	1983–87
Viles, Eliza Ann	Head Librarian	1975–80
Vishnevskaya, Galina	Visiting Voice Teacher	1991–97
Vittorini, Domenico	Italian and Italian Renaissance	1924–29; 1939–58
Vogelgesang, Frederick	Violin	1938–42
von Gronicka, Hilda	German Diction	1970–72
von Wymetal, Eric	Assistant in Operatic Acting	1931–32
von Wymetal, Wilhelm	Operatic Acting	1927–34

Name	Subject	Years
Walker, Elizabeth	Assistant Librarian Head Librarian	1977–80 1980–
Wallace, Emily M.	Literature and Composition	1977–84
Wallace, Robert	Tutor	1957–58
Walter, William E.	Director, The Curtis Institute of Music	1925–27
Walther, Madeleine	Voice	1925–27
Watson, Faith	English Literature	1996–
Watson, Mary E.	Supplementary Piano	1926–27
Weaver, John	Organ	1971–
Wedge, George	Theory	1924–26
Wehr, Mentzer	Science	1929–32
Weigand, Hermann J., Ph.D.	German	1924–29
Weiss, Piero	Supplementary Piano	1990–94
Wesner, Mary B.	Tutor	1927–50
Westmoreland, Elizabeth	Vocal and Opera Coach, Repertoire Music Director, Opera Department	1930–70 1957–67
Whiley, Helen W.	Theory	1925–26
Wightman, Florence	Harp	1926–27
Wiley, Peter	Violoncello	1996–
Wilson, Steuart	Voice, Vocal Ensemble, Repertoire	1939–41
Winn, Marjorie	Librarian	1928–35
Winslow, Helen	Accompanist, Coach	1925–35
Wittman, Jean Frois	French	1924–26
Woitach, Richard	Opera Coach, Conductor	1976–77
Woldin, Richard	Tutor	1973–74
Wolfson, Nessa	English for Foreign Students	1974–75
Wohlmuth, Hans, Ph.D.	Opera	1939–41; 1942–50
Woodhams, Richard	Oboe Orchestral Repertoire (Woodwinds)	1985– 1986–
Yahr, Barbara	Elements of Conducting	1985–90
Yannopoulos, Dino	Opera Head of Opera Department, Stage Director	1970–76 1976–77
Zambara, Edward	Voice	1995–98
Zaninelli, Luigi	Theory	1954–59
Zarzeczna, Marion	Supplementary Piano	1962–
Zechiel, Ernest	Theory	1928–33
Zetlin, Emanuel	Violin	1925–28
Zimbalist, Efrem	Violin Director, The Curtis Institute of Music	1928–68 1941–68
Zuckerman, Diane	Tutor Secondary School Division	1976–77 1979–80

APPENDIX III

The Curtis Institute of Music wishes to thank all of the photographers whose images helped to bring this history to life. Despite our best efforts, we were unable to identify all of the individuals responsible for the photographs in this book. If you can identify the photographers responsible for the uncredited images, please contact the Communications Office at The Institute so that we can update our records.

PHOTO CREDITS

Cover
Brownie Harris

Inside Front Cover
Don Tracy

Pre-Introduction
Jennifer Shamess

Page ii
David Wells

Page v
David Swanson

Page vi
Don Tracy

Page ix
Don Tracy

Page x
David Swanson

Page xiii
Jean Brubaker

Page xiv
David Swanson

Page xvii
David DeBalko

Pages xviii–xix
Jerome Lukowicz

Pre-Chapter 1
Unknown

Page 3
Kubey-Rembrandt

Page 4
Unknown

Page 5
Unknown

Page 6
Unknown

Page 7
Kubey-Rembrandt

Page 8
Unknown

Page 9
Unknown

Page 11
Unknown

Page 12
Unknown

Page 13
Unknown

Page 14
Unknown

Page 15
Kubey-Rembrandt

Page 16
Fritz Henle/
Black Star

Page 17
Retouched by
Kubey-Rembrandt

Page 18
Unknown

Page 19
From a drawing by
Ruyl

Page 20
Kubey-Rembrandt

Page 23
Unknown

Page 25
Unknown

Page 26
Fritz Henle/
Black Star

Page 28
Unknown

Page 30
Unknown

Page 31
Fritz Henle/
Black Star

Page 33
Fritz Henle/
Black Star

Page 36
S. F. Mack

Page 37
Unknown

Page 38
William R. Rittase

Page 42
Unknown

Page 45
Unknown

Page 46
Unknown

Page 49
Unknown

Pages 50–51
Tyler Fogg

Page 55
Unknown

Page 57
Photo Illustrators

Page 58
Unknown

Page 59
Henry Grossman

Page 60
Unknown

Page 62
Gilbert Silvestri

Page 65
Peter Checchia

Page 68
Don Tracy

Page 70
Peter Checchia

Page 72
Peter Checchia

Page 73
Unknown

Page 76
Julie Jensen

Page 78
Unknown

Page 81
I. George Bilyk

Page 82
Neil Benson

Page 83
Unknown

Page 84
Neil Benson

Page 85
I. George Bilyk

Page 87
I. George Bilyk

Page 88
Neil Benson

Page 89
I. George Bilyk

Page 90
Henry Grossman

Page 91
Unknown

Page 92
Neil Benson

Page 94
I. George Bilyk

Page 95
Neil Benson

Page 96
Alexander Agor

Page 98
Don Tracy

Page 101
David Swanson

Pages 102–103
PECO Energy
Company

Page 104
David Swanson

Page 105
David Swanson

Page 107
Jean Brubaker

Page 108
David DeBalko

Page 109
Don Tracy

Page 112
David Swanson

Page 113
Don Tracy

Page 114
Don Tracy

Page 115
Don Tracy

Page 116
Don Tracy

Page 117
David DeBalko

Page 118
Yvonne Unrath

Page 121
Chris Clark

Page 122
Don Tracy

Page 123
Don Tracy

Page 124
Don Tracy

Page 126
H. G. Haggerty

Page 127
Mitch Berger

Page 128
Don Tracy

Page 130
Don Tracy

Page 133
Don Tracy

Pages 134–135
Jerome Lukowicz